*Dedicated to the men and women
who settled the Plains.*

———————■———————

MY FOLKS CLAIMED THE PLAINS

A Treasury of Pioneer Stories
Handed Down in Families of Capper's Readers

Capper Press
Topeka, Kansas

Reprint Design and Production:
Diana J. Edwardson

Reprint Editor:
Michele R. Webb

ISBN: 0-941678-03-2

FOREWORD

In early 1955, the editors of *Capper's Weekly* (now *Capper's*), believing that word-of-mouth accounts of covered wagon days were in danger of being lost, asked readers to share pioneering experiences they had lived, or that had been handed down as stories in their families. The result was the 1956 publication of the book entitled "My Folks Came In A Covered Wagon."

In 1977, a request again went out to the readers of *Capper's Weekly*, this time for stories about life on early day homesteads. These stories are combined with others collected through the years for publication as a sequel to "My Folks Came In A Covered Wagon."

A terrific response led to the first printing of "My Folks Claimed the Plains" in 1978. Many readers put to paper the stories handed down in their families, and some of the writers actually experienced the hardships and pleasures of homesteading.

These accounts of claiming the Plains are a valuable contribution to preservation of Plains folklore. The character of the men and women who lived the stories make us proud we can claim them as ancestors, and that pride shines through the tales recounted by the sons, daughters and grandchildren of the homesteaders.

Capper Press is pleased to bring you a reprint of the original book of homesteading letters, with a new look on the outside that we think honors the brave settlers depicted inside. Again, this book is a sequel to "My Folks Came In A Covered Wagon," which has also been reprinted in its original form. We make no claim of historical accuracy, even admit that folktales tend to take on a little extra glow over the years. In an attempt to preserve the authentic flavor of the letters, the editors have made no spelling or punctuation corrections.

These stories are presented for your pleasure, with the hope that they allow a small glimpse into the times and the lives of the people who contributed so much to the strength of the Plains states. Our thanks and a salute to the contributors, who made this book possible for yet another generation of readers.

Visions

How varied the vision that led men to seek
The distant outposts when this land was young,
Some saw adventure that beckoned from afar,
while others, being gentle men, and meek,
Heard the call of land where low hills flung
Green crests against the sky, and followed the star
To tender grass and little friendly streams.
There were men who sought for gold, men bound to roam,
But women had a common bond to share,
They wrapped their tiny, precious seeds and dreams
And dared the wilderness to found a home,
To build a fence and set young gourd vines there.

—Alma Robison Higbee

CONTENTS

CHAPTER 1: That Promised Land!

Lured by Free Land

Attracted by the free land in Kansas, and the possibility that two young sons, too, could homestead or buy cheap farms in a few years, the Zerah Stedmans sold most of their possessions in 1870 and bought passage to the end of the railroad line at Nebraska City, Neb.

When their goods had been ferried across the Missouri River there, Zerah hired a driver with a wagon and oxen to carry the family to their claim in Marshall County, Kansas.

The oxen pulled the plow which cut the prairie sod, and the Stedmans built their first prairie home. The final job for the oxen and wagon was to deliver a ridge pole and shorter roof supports from timber on the creek. Then the Stedmans watched the wagon roll across the lonely prairie until it disappeared.

Zerah, once the transaction for the land was completed, found work at a mill 16 miles away. On Saturday afternoon he walked home and on Monday he walked the 16 miles back to work. Part of his wages was paid in flour and cornmeal, a great benefit to the family.

In the soddy, Phebe Stedman directed her boys to hoe out a shallow trench at the base of the walls, and in one corner she had dug a sinkhole, a little larger than a gallon pail. In case the side walls leaked in a driving rain and water threatened to muddy her

1

packed-dirt floors, the trench would collect the seepage and direct it to the sinkhole.

Always a neat and industrious homemaker, Phebe handsewed yards and yards of sheeting, brought from her Michigan home, to make a ceiling. It hid the poles and the sod overlay, and even better, it prevented dirt from sifting down. She also constructed a muslin wall to gain the privacy of a bedroom.

The boys were preparing for winter, too. They cut dried tall grass and twisted it so it would burn slowly and evenly in the stove.

How fortunate this family was! They had a snug house, food, fuel, and more land than they had ever hoped to own. I am happy to be kin to these pioneers. Zerah and Phebe Stedman were my great-grandparents.

> Mrs. Adolph Musil
> Home, Kan.

When 'Out West' Was Western 'York'

My great-great-grandparents, both born in New York State in 1791, decided to go to a new country after they were married and had a baby boy.

They hitched the oxen to a cart loaded with clothing, bedding, plow, spinning wheel—and the root of a sweetbriar rose.

They started "out west," but were still in "York" state when they found a lovely rich spot in the depths of thick forest with a fine spring, and decided this place would be their new home. They lived in the wagon while felling trees and hewing logs to make a cabin. Rocks around a fire were a place to set the spider for frying game and fish and for the coffeepot.

There were good friendly Indian neighbors, but no white people. The couple's seven-year-old son grew accustomed to seeing Indian women in blankets and feathers, and one day called to his mother, "Come, see, here is something which looks like you." Sure enough, he had seen a white woman wearing a dress and bonnet.

2

Wild game was plentiful, as was wild fruit. Bears, when they smelled honey in the house, would climb on the roof trying to find a way inside the cabin.

The young couple raised flax and harvested it by hand. The stems were retted, then flailed to separate the fibers which were cleaned, spun, and woven into cloth. After it was woven the cloth had to be bleached by being dipped in water and spread on the grass in sunshine until it was white as snow. Great-great-grandfather's summer suits were made of linen as was just about everything else for which white cloth was suitable.

Winter called for wools or linsey-woolsey, a coarse fabric which combined linen and wool. Big bolts of the cloth were prepared and the whole family had clothing made from the same material. All clothes were made by hand.

Once when making a coat, Great-great-grandmother broke the point off her needle. When her husband tried to sharpen it for her, he sharpened the eye instead of the point. The sewing stopped until he went to town—many miles away—to buy another needle.

All socks and mittens were knitted by hand. At butchering time, lacking jars for storage, the family put lard in a trough hewn from a log and covered it with a linen cloth.

Mrs Amy C. Shaw
Mound City, Kan. 66056

No Traveling on April Fools' Day

My great-grandfather Daniel Fitzgerald came to Iowa in the 1850s to escape the famine in Ireland. He lived all along the Mississippi River, from Keokuk to McGregor, finally settling at Harper's Ferry, Iowa. After the Civil War, he crossed the state to take up a farm in Pocahontas County, 40 miles from any town.

His party traveled thru spring rains in a wagon pulled by oxen. These pioneers carried with them squash, pumpkins, carrots, cabbage, salt pork, sugar, and coffee. Departure from Harper's Ferry was delayed a day, until April 2, because Great-grandfather refused to do anything on April Fools' Day unless he had to.

Wood was scarce and costly, and a customer who did not have the cash, that is gold or silver, did not buy. Flour, tea, salt, coffee, and other staples were sold for cash on the barrel head—or no sale! Grandfather had enough money to build a frame house and to put in a crop. He planted sod corn and about 20 acres of wheat the first year, and each year more ground was plowed until the land was all broken.

Ed Murphy
Fonda, Iowa 50540

Land Scout for the Family

I would like to tell you of my grandfather who came to Jackson, Neb., from St. Louis, on foot. He lived here with the Indians for many years.

After he had laid out where all his relatives could settle, he went back to St. Louis and told them what he had found. Some of his family took to their horses and came to see if he was right. Later their families came in covered wagons.

I am on the same place where my grandfather stopped. I have a horse barn that is made with pegs, no nails in the framework.

When I was small, Indians used to go west with horsedrawn wagons to their powwows, and they would water their horses and camp here. An Indian is a good friend if he likes you.

William F. Ryan
Route 2
Jackson, Neb. 68743

Smoke Signals Fooled Them

Alonzo Noble knew his sister and her family were coming to Nebraska, and as it happened, 160 acres across the road from his farm were available for homesteading. Alonzo was desirous of having his brother-in-law settle there.

On that land he threw up a shack, and if a covered wagon was seen coming over the hills, he would build a fire in the little hut.

4

As the wagon approached, smoke would come pouring from the chimney, and the driver, assuming someone lived there, would continue on his way.

And then the proper wagon appeared bringing the James Ostrander family from Wisconsin in 1865, and Alonzo's brother-in-law took immediate steps to file a claim on the land. And this is how, I am told, my great-grandparents came to own the last quarter section to be homesteaded in Johnson County, Nebraska.

Myron Reese
Farragut, Iowa 51639

The Claim That Grew and Grew

Bessie Reed Thomas arrived in Kansas in 1871, a bride of 18, with a shotgun across her knees. Her husband, William K. Thomas, a veteran of the Civil War, was coming west to settle on his soldier's claim, 160 acres in Ellis County.

In their two wagons they carried a Ben Franklin stove and provisions to last a year: a barrel of apples, flour, sugar, dried fruit, and smoked meat. One of their wedding gifts, a wonderful sewing machine, one of the first to be marketed, never arrived in Kansas; on the way the young groom had persuaded his wife to trade it for a cow, which was to be the beginning of their Hereford herd.

By fall the family had moved from the wagon to a new dugout. Bessie papered the dirt walls with copies of the *Louisville Courier*, and later, in 1879, she added a layer of the *Weekly Capital*, a paper that would later be named *Capper's Weekly*. The newspapers not only kept the dirt from falling into the room, but they served as a barrier to snakes, centipedes, scorpions, and the huge spiders common in that country.

Countless settlers had abandoned claims in Kansas. Indian massacres, tornados, blizzards, and grasshopper plagues had taken their toll, and an epidemic of diphtheria had wiped out entire families. To bring more settlers to the region, the government offered a deserted claim to anyone who would sleep on it for six months. A quarter section adjoining the Thomas's original claim was acquired in Bessie's name; she slept in a sod house there, a house similar to the one which now stood on her husband's claim as a replacement for the dugout.

The government made still another bid for new settlers, offering a timber claim to anyone planting and nurturing a thousand young trees on the land. To qualify for this additional claim of 160 acres, the Thomases traveled 16 miles to the Saline River bottoms to obtain cottonwood saplings which they planted and tended, hauling water from their windmill.

With this new claim they were the possessors of 480 acres of Kansas prairie—hardpan, buffalo grass, and tumbleweed, a plant Bessie often mistook for a crouching Indian.

The ranch continued to grow. William added 1,360 acres at a cost which was less than the asking price for one of those acres today. Between 1871 and 1899, he accumulated 2,200 acres.

A 10-room stone ranch house on the property was the birthplace of their sixth child, the writer of this account.

Marie Reed Thomas Titcomb
1831 West Algonquin Road
Hoffman Estates, Ill. 60195

The Sooner Had His Price

This story of the Fitzpatrick family's move to Oklahoma after the run of 1889 is part of a longer manuscript written by my mother, Iva Fitzpatrick Potter, when she was 91 years old. After the death of her mother when she was seven months old, the little girl lived with her grandparents for nearly 15 years. These recollections begin when she was seven years old:

My grandfather, Joseph J. Fitzpatrick, and my father, William W. Fitzpatrick, made the run to Oklahoma from Arkansas City, Kan., on April 22, 1889. They staked claims cornering, five-and-a-half miles southeast of Mulhall on Beaver Creek.

My father had been on his claim only a few hours when a man came by and said he had staked a claim on the land before Father did. Father knew he was a Sooner or claim jumper, as some called the men who came into the territory before it was officially opened. All they wanted was money or something that could be turned into money. Father offered him money—$25, I think. The man gladly took it, and Father never saw him again.

After the run, Father and Grandfather stayed on their claims so they could improve them. They had brought as many farming implements as they could carry in two wagons. They plowed up the sod, and planted pumpkins, potatoes, turnips, corn and other garden seeds. They dug wells and walled them with rock. Grandfather built a two-room cabin from oak logs which he and Father hewed so they would fit together closely; if there was a space between logs they chinked it with clay from the creek bed.

In October the men came back to Kansas to bring their families to Oklahoma. When we came to the Salt Fork, it was bankfull so we couldn't ford it. Some men had a ferry boat there which held a team and wagon. Horses on the bank pulled the ferry across by means of a heavy rope; men helped with their long poles. My uncles, on horses, drove the cows across.

The next stream we crossed was Red Rock, and as the wagon went down the bank to the stream, a barrel of pickles my grandmother was taking to her new home turned over. I cried as some pickles went floating downstream, but Grandfather lifted the barrel quickly and we didn't lose many.

There weren't any bridges for wagons over the creeks or rivers for a long time after Oklahoma was opened. The only bridges were built for trains. For the '89 run some men put boards down between the rails of the railroad bridges so horses and wagons could get to the starting points.

It took six days to make the trip from Cedar Vale, Kan., where we had lived, to the claims.

There were many wild animals when we came to Oklahoma. We saw bobcats, lynx, and early one evening we heard a panther. It was following along the creek and would scream once in a while, sounding like a person in trouble. We saw a few deer when they passed between the house and the creek; some hunters were after them, but lost track of them. One day Grandfather went across the creek to cut wood and a flock of turkeys came out of the trees. He shot one and we had it for our Thanksgiving dinner. The men always took a gun when they went to the woods or fields in hope they could shoot some game.

Grandmother and I went to Beaver Creek to pick plums and wild grapes. We also found greens such as lambsquarters, poke, dock and wild lettuce. They made good eating—if you like greens. We picked sheep sorrell to make filling for pie. It tasted like rhubarb.

Some men came to see Grandfather about locating a sawmill on the bank of Beaver Creek, a little distance from our house; Grandfather thought it would be fine. There were many trees on the creek and the men around the area could cut trees and bring them to the mill to be sawed into lumber. The owners of the mill took lumber in return for their services. So a lot of families were able to live in a house instead of in a dugout with a dirt floor. My father built a three-room house with lumber from the mill.

> Mrs. Thelma Potter Taylor
> Box 164
> Medford, Okla. 73759

Wagon Train West

One morning in early April, 1879, my parents, E. S. Wade and Hannah Landis Wade and their three children, and several other families of the La Harpe, Ill., vicinity set out by wagon train for Nebraska.

Each family had a large covered wagon in which their belongings and the children rode. They had wagons of food for themselves and their stock.

Each family took a milk cow or two, a sow, and some chickens, as well as plows and harrows and whatever else they could find room for.

Many families had at least one riding horse as well as a work team or two. The women took turns with their husbands driving the wagons and riding horseback.

As a child I heard stories of the hardships of their life in Nebraska. Most of the families were pretty tired of the struggle by the time they got their claims proved, so they sold their land and came back to Illinois.

Inez Wade Coleman
West Point, Iowa 52656

To a New Home by Rail and Wagon

After my father, W. C. Lewis, and my two married brothers, Lemuel and Gwynn, each filed on 640 acres of land in Moffat County, Colorado, in 1916, they returned to our home near Denver to tear down all the barns and salvage what lumber they could use at the new homestead. The wood was loaded in boxcars, along with the horses, cows, chickens, and all our possessions, and shipped by rail to Craig, Colo. The men traveled with the stock, to care for them, and my two sisters-in-law, Mother, and I, then about seven years old, rode the train over the old Moffat Road to Craig, Colo.

We all moved into a vacant cabin on the outskirts of Craig. We lived there until plans were completed for the 40-mile trip to the homestead and the wagons were loaded.

I remember how surprised I was when we drove to Craig for groceries and I saw the American flag. I thought we had left the United States.

My folks knew of two vacant cabins on Timber Lake Draw, not far from our new land, so that was the place we headed for, always watching Baker's Peak and the Black Mountains ahead of us. The roads were terrible. I remember how frightened Mother was when a hayrack, loaded with furniture, turned over. She thought Gwynn, who was driving, would be hurt, but he had jumped and saved himself.

We had been warned in Craig about the danger of ticks. We were advised always to carry a bottle of turpentine and to touch the ticks with turpentine when they stuck to the skin. One morning I found a tick on my leg and I knew that was the last of me. After a big commotion the tick was removed and we were on our way. But I grew sick, and my folks, inquiring of other homesteaders they happened to meet, heard them say I had mountain fever. I recall we stopped to water the horses at the Herring homestead but I remember nothing more of the trip until Father carried me into the cabin.

Mother gathered sagebrush roots to burn in our stove and Father made a bitter tea from the sage leaves and he was able to get some down me. Then my sister-in-law came from the other cabin, across the ravine, where my brothers' families were living, and said Gwynn was sick with the same symptoms I had. Lemuel and his wife rode horseback to Baggs, Wyo., 12 miles away, to get a doctor. He came in his Model T coupe. I heard him whisper to my parents that I was going to die. When Mother came to my bed, I said, "Don't you believe it. I am going to live." I got better fast, as did Gwynn.

Work started on building the cabins on the three homesteads. It was delayed once as Father and Lemuel stopped to put up a fence that would hold our cows and horses. Mother's and my work was to herd the three milk cows, but one day while we were eating our dinner, they disappeared. Gwynn saddled a horse and took out to find them. He was gone several days and finally located them at the edge of the forest reserve. Had they wandered into the reserve, he never would have found them for the trees were so dense there.

Our cabin had a kitchen, a front room, and two little bedrooms. Lemuel's and Gwynn's cabins each had one big room and a lean-to kitchen. We were glad to move from the little cabins on Timber Lake Draw because their doby roofs leaked rain.

The men started to dig water wells. Gwynn found water on his claim, but Lemuel and Father failed so they had to haul water. Later Lemuel moved his cabin, with its beautiful view of Baker's Peak and the Black Mountains, to the valley where he had a spring and a well.

Next came the horse barns. Father, my brothers and their

wives, hauled lumber and logs from the mountains where there was a sawmill.

In the early spring, the job of cleaning the ground of sagebrush began. The men tried everything to dig the sage out. Finally, with a John Deere tractor, they succeeded in breaking 100 acres on Father's place and 60 acres on each of the boys' places.

They planted wheat and that year it thrashed out 10 bushels to an acre. It was a big job just trying to keep the gophers and jackrabbits from eating the grain, altho the government furnished poisoned oats for their control.

The men decided that the country was too dry for grain crops, so they would raise stock and grow only enough feed to bring them thru the winter. There was a lot of open range for grazing. Father bought 500 head of sheep. Lemuel bought cattle, and Gwynn raised pigs.

After the sheep arrived, Mother and I herded them, following them all over the range with our dogs. Father built two long sheds and a large pen, and we brought the sheep in every night. We always had a horse or two to ride, for the sheep would go far to find grass. One day they ran several miles in a hailstorm before Mother and I could head them off.

Another time when we were on the range with the sheep, we were in a big rainstorm, a regular cloudburst. We could hear the roar of water, and looking up Timber Lake Draw, we could see it coming toward us. Mother and I hurried the sheep across the draw to the side where we lived. The water was black, carrying old lumber from a gold miner's camp upstream and sagebrush; it filled the draw bank to bank, about four feet deep.

When Mother and I found beautiful rocks we brought them home to put around our cabin and cave. We also brought in deer horns, buffalo horns and cactus plants. Our cave was a real showplace. The flowers in summer were beautiful—Indian paintbrush, bluebells, morning-glories—so many I cannot name them all.

Mrs. Kittie Ann Hickman
Rawlins, Wyo. 82301

Diphtheria Marred Arrival in Wyoming

My parents and we three little girls were living in Iowa when the lure of land in the West, free for our settling there and improving it, proved too much for our dad. He, along with other men from Iowa and our Uncle Frank, went west to the wild plains, without a tree, with nothing but buffalo grass and sagebrush.

It was the year 1908 when my parents decided to make the move. The horses, one cow, chickens, household goods, machinery, and our dog Bessie were shipped by railroad. Dad traveled with the animals to take care of them. Mother and we girls went on the passenger train.

On the train, I came down with diphtheria, and when we arrived at Pine Bluffs, Wyo., we were moved into a small house and quarantined there—no one could go out or come in. Our dad decided to stay with his family until I was well.

So all our belongings had to be taken care of. It was lucky for us that Uncle Frank had been there long enough to have his place improved, so he and some friends from Iowa took our things to their home to care for them.

The men, with Uncle Frank in charge, built a barn and started a house for us.

Dad had to have a well drilled; our well was over 300 feet deep. He put up a windmill to pump water and made a tank to hold a reserve supply. He had to make fences and plow the ground, and it took good horses on a breaking plow to turn that land. We made a sod house for our chickens, and Mother had a garden. She planted a yellow rose bush she had brought from Iowa, and the little thing lived all those bad winters.

All the families raised hogs and cattle and butchered and cured meat. Fruit was shipped in by rail to Pine Bluffs. Everyone went to get some for winter. Dad would take a load of wheat to the elevator and bring back a load of apples. We had a big cellar, and the apples rated a bin of their own.

We lived far from town so there was no doctor near us. Dad and Mother took care of us children. If we took a cold, we got turpentine and lard rubbed on the chest and neck, and an old black stocking was wrapped around our neck. Dad also kept a bottle of whiskey—for medicine only. We sipped a hot toddy for anything from a sick stomach to the flu.

For entertainment, the families would gather at a home and have an old-fashioned dance. We kids were put to bed in a bedroom. All the women took a cake or some other food for refreshments.

Farming was a hard way of life. Sometimes there would not be enough rain, and when it did rain, we might also have a big hailstorm which ruined the wheat crop. The winters with the blizzards were terrible; we often lost cattle in the sudden storms when the cows could not get to the cattle sheds. They would huddle together and some would die.

When my folks could take no more, they sold out and moved to Missouri— many years ago.

> Mrs. Harry Stanley
> 514 South Halliburton
> Kirksville, Mo. 63501

A Nebraska Saga

My father, John Steinke, lived 83 years in Perkins County, Nebraska, before his death in 1977. Some years ago he wrote an account of life on his father's homestead, a story which spanned 30 years from 1883, when the claim was filed, to about the time of World War I, when the character of farming, as he knew it, was changing with the introduction of big farm machines.

The following paragraphs are based on material in my father's original manuscript:

After my dad, Louis Steinke, filed on a homestead northeast of Verango, Neb., he returned to Buffalo County to await the next year's spring when he would bring his wife, in a covered wagon, to Perkins County (or Keith County as it was called then). They lived in the wagon until a 12- by 16-foot frame shack could be completed.

13

Dad helped build the High Line Railroad thru west Nebraska. He drove mules hitched to a scraper to smooth the grade for the tracks. After two years he had saved a little money and in 1888 he was able to replace the shack with a two-room sod house. The first child born to the family died and was buried on the homestead, for there were no cemeteries in the area at the time of his death. All the other children in the family were born and reared on that farm.

When the horses which had pulled his wagon West died, he bought a yoke of oxen which he used to break sod. The oxen also made weekly trips to Big Springs for the family's water which was hauled home in barrels. None was ever wasted, so we all washed in the same water.

Later Dad traded those oxen for horses, and after one died and he had no money to buy a replacement, he broke a milk cow to work with a horse as a team.

The years of 1894-1896 were trying times. In 1894, the drouth was bad; the corn grew only about a foot before it burned up. Dad put clothes in a sack and walked to Greeley, Colo., where he picked potatoes, earning money so we could eat thru the winter.

The next spring was dry, too. Dad sowed spring wheat; it didn't sprout. He sowed oats; they didn't come up. And then he planted corn. In June a little rain fell, and wheat, oats, and corn all came up together.

That year Dad had some pigs, but he had raised no feed for them and he could not find any feed in the country. He took them to Ogallala, where he did his trading, hoping he could sell them. When no sale was possible, he drove into an alley and turned them loose. Someone, he hoped, would pick them up and feed them.

When the drouth broke after several successive dry years, the rains came and crops grew better. But new hazards appeared. The area suffered hail-outs several times. And then the grasshoppers came. The pests ate everything in sight: all the foliage, curtains at the windows—just about ate the harness off the horse's back!

Before the dry years there were three or four families on every

14

other section (the alternate sections were railroad land then). By late 1896 so many families had left that there were only five left in our township.

The antelopes in herds of 25 or more came to the range around our soddy. We children used to chase them. Never caught a one!

We walked to school about 3^1/$_2$ miles northwest of our home. If the weather was so bad that we couldn't walk, we stayed at home; nobody took us to school. To keep our feet warm on cold days we wrapped grain sacks around our shoes.

In those days we had only three months of school, for there was little money to pay the teacher. At that rate it took years to get thru the eighth grade, and it was nothing for kids of 18 or 20 years old to be going to school.

Butchering was a big winter job. Every family rendered lard, and cured and smoked ham, shoulder and bacon. We saved the intestines of animals, and cleaned them by pouring water thru them and scraping. When they were thin, they were suitable for sausage casings. We slipped the casing over a piece of cow horn, and holding the horn in one hand, we used the other hand to stuff the sausage into the casing. We made blood sausage, liver sausage, and several other kinds. They were tied like modern-day bologna sausages and smoked.

About 1901 Dad put down a well. It was drilled by horse power and took nearly a year to complete. With a water supply at hand, Dad began to add cattle.

It was my job to watch the cattle and sometimes I walked miles to find them. Rattlesnakes were numerous; it was nothing to kill six or more a day. I walked barefooted because there was no money for shoes, and since I could not see the snakes in the tall grass I was often scared. It is surprising that none of us was ever bitten. Cactuses were plentiful, too, and they are hard on bare feet.

We milked 15 cows usually. We strained the milk into gallon crocks, let them stand for a day, and skimmed off the cream. The crocks had to be emptied and washed every day. We churned butter and sold it in town.

To go to Grant, we used to straightline across the prairie from our farm to the town. There were no roads, only cow trails. People traveled directly to their destination because there were no barriers to prevent their doing so.

Most of the land was free range and the cattle all ran together. In the fall everyone rounded up his cattle. Dad ran about 80 head of horses and several hundred head of cattle. There were big ranches to the west and south of us.

About the time of World War I, the ranchers and farmers began to buy big tractors and other machinery. They broke up the prairie and planted wheat. We had to sell our cattle and horses for what we could get for them for there no longer was open pasture. We, too, became wheat farmers.

Mrs. Clifford Winterquist
Box 352
Grant, Neb. 69140

Waiting for the Run

I remember the opening of the Cherokee Strip in 1893. Registration booths were put up near my father's house which was about two miles south of Caldwell, Kan., on the Kansas line.

Seven men from Washington took care of the booths. They told my father to bring his papers over when they were ready to accept registrations and he could be the first to sign.

Men stayed in line all day and night as they were afraid they would lose their place if they should leave. My brother took them coffee and sandwiches.

My mother and sister cooked for the men from Washington. They liked chicken, so they had chicken every day. They paid 24 cents a meal, and when they left they gave Mother a $100 bill.

It was like a town all around our house. There was a barbershop, a restaurant, an ice cream stand and other stands. When the shot was fired to signal the opening of the strip, people rushed away in buggies, covered wagons, on horseback and on foot. They got water from our well for their horses and filled cans until the well was dry.

My father staked a claim, put a flag up, and left for a little while. When he returned he found a man had taken the flag down and put up his own. The intruder was convinced he should leave.

Mrs. Ada Ball
Cabool, Mo. 65689

'Let's Go Home!'

When the line was formed for the race to the Cherokee Strip, Dad was there on a pony. Mother was somewhere back of the line with her five children, the youngest a six-week-old baby, in a covered wagon. They had agreed that their meeting place after the race would be a certain lone tree on the prairie. As soon as the racers were out of sight, Mother drove to the tree, and there she waited out the long day. Soon after sunset, Dad rode up to the wagon and greeted his family with "Come on! Let's go home!"

That first night they slept in the wagon, but the next day they put up a tent which was to be their home that summer. In the fall, neighbors, working together, cut timber and put up log cabins for their families. The cabin was my parents' home for eight years.

The first winter Dad wore gunny sacks tied on his feet; there was no money for shoes. He would cut a load of wood, haul it 20 miles to town, sell it, and bring home what groceries the money would buy.

In some way they came to own an old red cow with long horns and a mean disposition. One day Dad went to town with wood and left the cow lariated to a tree. When he was late coming home, Mother decided to milk her. The cow had a different idea; she lowered her horns and made for Mother. Round the tree Mother went, the cow right behind her; round and round they went until the rope was used up. When Bossy could go no further, she decided she was well tied and allowed Mother to take enough milk to feed the children at supper.

The cabin had only one door and one window. Mother, who cooked on a wood stove, often complained that the cabin was hot. Dad just as often promised her that as soon as the field work was done, he would put a door in the other end of the cabin. One day during dinner Mother again mentioned the heat. Dad said, "Why don't you cut a door in the other end?" Mother had no answer for him. But when he came from the field that night, the cabin had an unorthodox second door. Dad was forced to delay his field work to make a door to fit the hole Mother had cut.

Mrs. Paul Laubach
Quenemo, Kan. 66528

A Camp for Spectators

I was 11 years old at the time of the big run into the Cherokee Outlet. My father, grandfather, and uncle made the trip to Cameron, Kan., on the state's boundary, and stood in line for several days before they could register. They never left the line, day or night, because they would lose their places.

Mother, Grandmother, Brother, and I went with a neighbor's family in their wagon to see the run. We camped on Big Sandy Creek, just west of where Waldron, Kan., is now. Hundreds of people camped there, some with their cows. The men sank a wooden box in the creek sand and water came up in it for the horses to drink. We went west to a place south of Kiowa to see the start of the run. Such a big rush! Some were on horses, many were in wagons.

In Oklahoma, my father staked a claim which cornered on school land, and we moved from near Harper to the strip in 1894, with everything we had—three cows, hogs, and a few chickens.

Our community had no school until 1895, and that year we had only a three-month term. I rode three miles to school on an old work horse without a saddle, and as all girls did then, I rode sideways.

For social gatherings, we had spelling matches, box suppers, and school programs.

Mrs. Fannie Soper
Manchester, Okla. 73758

Adventure Was a Lure

Why would my parents claim land? My mother's answer was, "Why not?" She and my father were young; they wanted to get ahead. Adventure itself was a lure. And my father had a longing for land, a longing that was to stay with him all of his life.

So they filed on land near Nolan, S.D., in 1907, and set forth with their two children to live their adventure.

Some years later my mother wrote about their arrival at the claim:

"In our hired wagon we set out from Pierre and we drove for miles over the hills without seeing a sign of human life. The hills were not enormous, but just rolling, rolling green land.

"To file a claim it was necessary to sign a contract with the government to take 160 acres and make them 'home.' A house must be built, a well dug, a certain number of acres plowed and a certain number of acres fenced in. We had two choices in obtaining the final deed: We could stay eight months and then pay some cash; or we could stay two years and pay no cash. We planned to stay the shorter time.

"Across the lonely land we drove, for hours and hours, and then suddenly there was our home!

"It had been built to order and we had not seen it before. Compared to other homesteaders' shacks (all houses were called shacks), it was large. Our house measured 12 by 16 feet.

"Bright, new, unpainted, it stood. A short distance away was a bright new unpainted outhouse. There was nothing else in any direction.

"The house was built against a hill, with a door facing the east. It had one window, this on the south wall. We didn't need more windows. If there had been one in the back, it would have faced nothing but the side of the hill.

"Inside the walls were unfinished, with two-by-fours raw against the rose-colored building paper that lined the siding.

"We spread out our furnishings: a fullsize bed, and a second spring and mattress which John hinged so that in the daytime it hung against the wall. There was a dresser, a kitchen safe, a table and chairs, a rocker, my sewing machine, a stove, and enough green lightweight carpeting to cover half the floor."

This was home! And thus began the John and Lillian Sherk adventure in homesteading.

Lucile Houser
Route 17, Box 86
Tyler, Texas 75704

Quick Cure for Pioneering Fever

When our century was young, there was still government land in Kansas to be given to people with "pioneering fever." In the summer of 1908, my parents had an attack of that malady and decided it was time they should own their own farm.

Some friends who had bought a relinquishment in Kansas sent back letters full of hope for the future. After the threshing was over, my parents had a few hundred dollars which they planned to use either for filing a claim or for buying a relinquishment.

Father insisted Mother and I go with him to this land of promise, so on a hot Sunday in mid-August we boarded a train and headed for the far corner of Kansas.

We arrived at the town shortly after noon and walked to the hotel with a scorching sun bearing down on us. At the hotel we were served a meal of leftovers. Then Father hired a driver with a team and surrey to take us to the home of our friends.

Those were the longest 15 miles I ever traveled. The sun beat down on our backs and the heat was almost unbearable. The horses struggled thru sand while sweat dripped from their bodies. Up hill and down we went, seeing no signs of life on that road until we came to a sod house. In a group of people sitting on the ground in the shade of the house, we recognized our friends. Father paid the driver, and we joined the party. They gave us drinks of water from a barrel which sat in the shade of the house; it was wet but not cool. When the group broke up, we were loaded into a wagon to ride a few more miles to our hosts' home.

Our friends, who had a little money when they moved to this area, were better equipped to face the hardships of frontier life than were many of their neighbors. They had a well and a windmill, a two-room frame house and a cave.

Our hostess built a roaring fire in the cookstove using "Kansas coal" and prepared supper for eight.

While the hour grew late, we were all bedded down for the night. Mother and I were given the bed and Father slept on a pallet on the floor. Our friends and their children went to the cave to sleep.

Plans were made for us to go the next day to see a relinquishment which we were interested in buying. But when morning came Father had the lumbago so bad he couldn't get off his pallet without help. His only thought was to get back home where he would be near a doctor.

We were soon loaded in a wagon and headed for town where we met the train that carried us back to our comfortable rented home. Our pioneering fever had been cured.

Esther Billings Lamont
Route 2
Nevada, Mo. 64772

CHAPTER 2: Prairie Architecture

Soddy With Plastered Wall, Painted Floor

When Dad and Mother Bader made the journey to free land, they came not by wagon but by ship. They left their German village near Odessa in Russia in 1911 for a long and trying sea voyage. After arriving in America, there was another trying trip, this one by train, before they reached their destination in northwest Kansas. Here they were able to secure some farmland and build a two-room sod house.

Mother Bader was a particular housekeeper and liked things to be nice. When the house was finished, she made a smooth mix of horse manure and mud and plastered this on the walls. Then she whitewashed it. Halfway up the wall around the cooking area she tacked patterned oilcloth which she could easily wipe clean.

She made a plaster to cover the dirt floor in the bedroom-parlor, then she painted the floor and added a fancy border. The floor, I was told, held up well and could be swept easily.

Shortly after the family was settled in the soddy, the women of the neighborhood held an afternoon housewarming. Most of the guests brought gifts of food; one woman brought a setting hen and some eggs. The most touching gift was that of a very poor woman whose husband was ill. She and her children had gathered a wagonload of prairie fuel (cow chips), and this gift, so much appreciated, brought tears to Mother Bader's eyes.

Dad Bader liked America as soon as he saw it and he never changed his mind. But Mother Bader's oldest daughter told me she often saw her mother crying in those early years. The family had given up so much to come to Kansas; the work was so hard; the future was uncertain; and there was no way she could ever go back home again.

Mrs. Robert Bader
Doniphan, Neb. 68832

Bark-covered Cabin

Grandfather Silas W. Condit built his house of logs covered with bark from cottonwood trees. The door of split logs was held together by wooden pegs and the fireplace was laid of sod. There were no windows. The time was 1848; the place was the junction of the Missouri and the Little Sioux rivers.

The family's provisions were what they could raise, shoot, or catch in the streams. Clothing was made from skins which Grandfather tanned. When he was elected justice of the peace, he performed his first marriage ceremony in a new buckskin suit. He had killed the deer, tanned the hide, and sewed the suit with sinews from the deer's spine.

Grandfather had a corn mill operated by a crank turned by hand that held about a peck of shelled corn. It was known as "Condit's Mill" by the neighbors who came from miles around to grind their grist.

J. E. Condit
Hagerman, Idaho 83332

He Built Good Housing for Family and Stock

My two older brothers came first, in 1899, with my uncle to his homestead in Sheridan County, Kansas, and in January of 1900 my father followed. He loaded a railroad car with livestock and machinery and left his home in Adair County, Iowa. When he had built a nice sod house on his homestead, a 160-acre farm nine miles south of Hoxie, Kan., Mother and the four younger children came by train to Selden, Kan., where he met us and took us to our new home. I was six months old.

I will try to describe the house Father built. It was made of sod and had three rooms with a pantry off the kitchen. Our kitchen had two windows, one on the west and one on the south, and on the east Father hung the outside door with a four-pane window in it. Mother had a nice coal range, a long dropleaf table, a cupboard with a glass door, a jelly cupboard with a screen door, and at the west window a big Morris chair.

Our kitchen, pantry, and bedroom had wooden floors, but our middle room had a dirt floor. It was spread with straw and covered with paper, and over that she laid a rag carpet tacked to 1-by-4s fitted around the walls. The carpet was taken up every spring, put on the clothesline, and beat to get all the dust out. Then new straw and papers were put down and the carpet was relaid.

The middle room had a window on the east wall and a double window on the west, and Mother had beautiful plants in all the windows. My folks slept in this room. Besides the bed, the room held Mother's dresser, an organ, two rocking chairs, and a little table. In the winter a two-lid topsy stove sat in the middle of the room; Mother did lots of cooking on it to save fuel.

The bedroom was divided by a rug tacked to make a "wall" thru the middle. My brothers slept on one side, we girls on the other. There were no closets, and all our clothes hung on the walls.

The barn was dug in a bank and faced the south so that end was made of lumber. The north side was built up about three feet higher than ground level, and big doors on leather hinges covered the openings there where hay was dropped to the horses. There were stalls for about 12 horses.

We had an open shed dug in the bank and covered with old hay. Father had a granary built of lumber; it had three big bins. He raised lots of chickens and kept them in two large sod henhouses.

East of the house Father dug a cave. We milked quite a few cows and kept the milk cool in the cave. Mother skimmed the cream from crocks and she churned and sold butter. The milk was fed to the calves and pigs.

In the fall my father would buy several bushels of apples as well as potatoes and cabbage for kraut, and these were kept in the cave. The cave smelled so good when I went down there in the winter.

When fall came, my father fixed side boards on the wagon and took all of us to the pasture to pick up cow chips. He would haul in two big loads and store the chips in part of one henhouse so they would stay dry. The chips and a big load of coal were our winter's fuel.

We had a deep well, 240 feet, that wouldn't pump dry. It filled the 100-gallon round wooden tank from which we irrigated the garden as well as the shallow pond where the ducks paddled. Everyone on the way to Hoxie watered tired horses at our well and treated himself to a cold drink. And, of course, he visited awhile if we were at home. No one was ever turned away from my father's house. Most peddlers, it seemed, arrived at noon or at evening, and many stayed all night.

We went visiting on Sundays, and I never knew my father to go to the fields or to work on that day. We had church in the schoolhouse on Sunday, literary meetings there, usually on Friday nights, and once each winter a box supper.

We children walked two miles to school, altho when it was stormy, someone might take us in the wagon. Every day, at noon, two of the pupils walked a quarter mile to fetch fresh drinking water for the teacher and the children.

Mary Dickinson
Fulton, Kan. 66738

Cozy Quarters

My family was one of three who took up adjoining homesteads in Dewey County, Oklahoma. We had a one-room shack on our place where the other families parked until they could build homes for themselves.

One family built a dugout with a dirt roof, but in that first winter the snows drifted high and the wind was so strong it blew in the front of the dugout. They came back to live with us.

By that time, all three families had increased by one baby each, and there were nine children and six grown-ups sleeping in that little shack, so we kept plenty warm. We had pallets all over the floor. Some of us older children were put in the loft; our fathers lifted us up thru a little hole in the ceiling.

Mrs. Ethel McAlary Lasater
Myrtle Creek, Ore. 97457

Reason To Rejoice

Our covered wagon rolled into Oklahoma Territory when I was two years old. My parents homesteaded a claim on a sandy 160 acres.

For seven years our home was a 12- by 16-foot half dugout. For five of those years we had a wall-to-wall dirt floor, and I remember my brother and I celebrating the completion of our new board floor. We ran back and forth and clapped our hands until the rest of the family got into the act. Dad hugged Mother, and she cried tears of joy. Then they thanked the Lord for our good fortune.

Is it any wonder that I remember?

Mrs. Bobbie L. Kennard
Sulphur Springs, Ark. 72768

Dugout Had a Porch

When Grandpa Jackson Brown built his family's first home in Kansas, he chose a location in a creek bank, high enough to escape flood waters, yet close to three springs. The springs would provide abundant water for drinking and cooking, and the creek would supply water for washing clothes and for other necessities.

A room about 8 by 12 feet was cut into the bank. The walls were straight and smooth and the dirt floor was level. Sod was used to extend the walls about two feet higher than ground level on three sides, and to construct the fourth wall which was pushed out from the lip of the bank about three feet to make the dugout larger. One window and a door were cut into the front wall which was nearly two feet thick.

The roof was made of saplings laid close together across a ridge log, covered with cornstalks or brush, and topped with a heavy layer of sod which would shed the rain.

Grandpa's dugout was fancier than most dugouts for the roof pole was long enough to create a porch roof which was supported by poles cut from small trees. Knowing Grandpa, I suspect he laid a porch floor. The porch was large enough to hold a barrel of pork and other things which were better kept outside the small house.

Furniture pieces were a stove, table and chairs, a safe for food and dishes, a bed, and a trundle bed for the children. The trundle bed could be pushed under the large bed during the daytime to be out of the way.

Emma Crabb
2012 Washburn
Topeka, Kan. 66611

Parchment Window

Grandfather wanted air and light in his dugout, but he had no glass for a window. At that time, merchants wrapped parcels in sheets of heavy brown paper about a yard square and folded in the middle. Grandfather greased a sheet of that paper to let in more light and tacked it over the opening as a substitute for glass.

Fuel was a problem for early settlers. Grandfather hitched a team to a wagon and drove across the prairie, which had neither roads or fences, looking for fuel. He and his children gathered weeds, antelope and buffalo horns, cow chips—anything that would burn.

The fuel was stored in a dry place, when it was time to cook a meal, a supply was brought in and placed by the cast iron stove. All food was then made ready, the fire was lighted, and one child was placed by the stove to feed the fire until the food was cooked.

Not much fuel was required for warmth because the dugouts were easily heated.

Mrs. Mabel Hawman
1706 Huxley Avenue
Monte Vista, Colo. 81144

Running Water in the Kitchen

In one end of the kitchen in our sod house in Holt County, Nebraska, we had an artesian well with constantly flowing water, winter and summer. It ran into a long wooden trough with a sliding shelf for butter, milk, eggs and other foods that needed cooling. It overflowed into an underground pipe which filled the stock tank in the barn lot and then to another overflow which sent the water to an open ditch and a pond.

Our house was a large soddy, and as I remember it in 1901 when my memories start, it was swanky for its time and place. It had real plastered walls and wooden floors, and a white muslin ceiling which was laid across the beams and was taken down from time to time for washing.

The house had five rooms: a large kitchen-dining room, sitting room, and three bedrooms.

Our outbuildings consisted of a dandy two-holer, a chickenhouse and a smokehouse, all made of sod with sod roofs. For livestock we had a long shed constructed of willow poles and woven wire covered with straw and rough coarse swamp grass, and for horses, a barn, the only frame building on the place.

Carl W. Moss
2112 Harlan Street
Denver, Colo. 80214

Door, Window Frames and Furniture for $7

In 1919 I married a young sergeant just discharged from the Army after World War I. The week after our marriage my husband filed on a homestead in northwestern Colorado. We both worked diligently thru the next six months, saving every penny for our move. In May we loaded our little Ford and traveled to our 320 acres.

With two other ex-service men who were homesteading in the area, my husband went to Douglas Mountain and cut trees for our cabin. It was a lovely cabin, 24 by 36 feet. As the logs were brought in, I stripped off the bark with a large spike. The men notched them for a tight fit, then as the logs for the roof were put in place, the bark was firmly packed between them and a layer of sod was placed on top.

My husband took some logs he had cut to a sawmill and had them cut into boards, enough to frame three windows and to make a door, a table and a bench—all for $7.

In that country the door was hung to swing inward, and one morning I opened the door and stood face to face with a big longhorn bull. How quickly I shut that door! The bull was as frightened as I was; he took off in a run.

With a 50-gallon barrel in the back of our Ford pickup, we drove seven miles to a neighbor's farm for water. We dipped water from his well with a bucket, and when the barrel was full, we turned a washtub over the top and drove home with a supply for drinking, laundering and dishwashing.

We planted a small garden, some corn and potatoes. It was a great surprise to see how fast it grew. Because we didn't bring any seed potatoes, we cut the eyes out of our eating potatoes and planted them. Those peelings yielded 28 bushels of potatoes.

Mrs. Elizabeth Fisher
Route 1
Great Bend, Kan. 67530

Back To the Old Stack

As a young man of 20, my husband went to western Kansas. His place did not have any buildings; it was just open prairie. He chose a spot near a draw with running water, mowed some grass, and put up a haystack. He burrowed into the side of the stack for shelter. He took a dozen chickens with him and lived on the eggs and what game he could shoot. He put up a shelter for horses and chickens and started a house of stone.

The evening he finished the house and moved in a storm came up. Lightning struck the house and ran down the chimney. It stunned him as he lay asleep a few feet from the chimney and blackened his silver knives and forks that were near the fireplace.

When he awoke the next morning and realized what the lightning had done, he moved back to the haystack.

Mrs. J. A. Winsor
Burlingame, Kan. 66413

Decor in Leafy Green

The winter my father and mother moved to Chapman, Kan. nearly 90 years ago, they found no place to live. So Father and my uncle built us a dugout out on the Smoky River.

My mother put a curtain in the one big room to make a bedroom and a kitchen. My father built a summer living room in a row of cottonwoods.

The dugout was warm in winter and cool in summer. My sister and I played with our shepherd dog on the dugout roof—it was grass as our father had covered the dugout with sod.

Young folks, friends of my step-sister, had picnics among the trees and went rowing on the river.

Mrs. John French
Box 71
Parma, Idaho 83660

Time Out for Hunting

My daddy and his brother worked together improving their places in Dewey County, Oklahoma, and lived in a covered wagon while they built their house.

Turning the sod with a team of horses and a sod plow, cutting it to workable lengths, hauling it on a sled made from logs, and stacking it to the proper height for walls took many days and a lot of work.

They chopped down a large tree with an ax for the ridge pole. Small trees cut for rafters were covered first with brush, then with cut grass, and then with dirt thrown over the brush and straw.

At the windows they tacked hides or whatever they could get ahold of.

They had to take time out to hunt for their food. They shot wild game, such as turkeys and pheasants, or if lucky, perhaps a buffalo.

By the time my daddy and uncle finished, they had three sod houses. Daddy, his brother, their mother and sister, all took up claims a mile apart down Cottonwood Creek.

Some time later a neighbor built a sawmill, and the men cut down big cottonwoods and dragged them to the mill. They cut enough lumber to cover the roofs and to build some outbuildings for stock.

Mrs. Art Marler
Mutual, Okla. 73853

Real Togetherness!

Our family of seven, plus an uncle and a cousin who came with us, arrived in Kansas in January, 1880. There was only a granary and one straw shelter on our land. Father hired three carpenters and while the men built the big barn and later the house, 12 of us lived in the 14- by 16-foot granary.

At nightfall, nine of us slept, crosswise, on our two bedsteads, resting our feet on chairs or boxes. The carpenters slept on a floorbed of blankets under our table.

When my parents got up at dawn, the carpenters crowded into the bed vacated by Father and Mom. Mom had to prepare breakfast and set the table, and there was no floor space for sleeping men. After the men ate and left for work, the rest of us got up.

I was just a little girl and I found pleasure in playing with pieces of discarded lumber and listening to the men sing and joke. They fitted boards and drove nails from early morning until dusk, pausing only at mealtimes.

Eva Vincent
Box 29
Alden, Kan. 67512

Wagon Home Needed for Job

Because of the bad drouth in 1901, my parents sold out in Missouri and went to Woodward, Okla. Father, Mother, and four children had to live in a covered wagon about two months because there was no house to rent—and no money to pay the rent if a house had been there.

Father had to have the wagon to haul brick, so he set the overjet and cover off on the ground and that was our only home, rain or shine, cold or hot. And it was mostly very cold! Covered wagons were heated by a small two-lid topsy stove in the front. A heavy canvas or quilt hung across the front of the wagon as a door.

My father and I hauled all the brick to build a store building in Woodward. We finished in 1902. Father earned 50 cents a day for himself and team, and I, age nine, received five cents a day. And a day's work was from daylight to dark. We furnished our own horse feed and our own eats.

Bennie Cashes Dockum
650 North Losrobes Avenue
Pasadena, Calif. 91101

Okie 'dobe

We lived in a tent and a small shack after we came to Oklahoma in 1907. On Thanksgiving Day of that year we moved into a new adobe home, 16 by 24 feet.

The adobe blocks were made on the farm. The virgin sod was

plowed, then disced. Water and a small portion of soil were worked with a spade and hoe into a very tough mixture. The mud mix was packed firmly into a hardwood mold, 8 by 12 by 16 inches, and let stand a few minutes before it was cut loose from the sides, and the mold could be lifted from the block. The adobe block was not moved until it was dry enough to turn, then each day it was turned until it was dry on all sides.

The blocks were laid like bricks in a wall, with mud as mortar.

Ten years later three more rooms with adobe walls were added, and the house was plastered inside and stuccoed outside. It still stands in 1978.

Fern Pounds
Elmwood, Okla. 73935

CHAPTER 3: Utilities Were Homemade

Tail Lights

My pioneer father came to Kansas from France in 1874. Reaching Hutchinson he purchased two wild steers, hitched them to an old wagon and started for his brother's dugout. There were no roads and the grass was higher than the oxen's backs. Rags tied to the tips of the grass marked the trail.

My father and his brother built a house on the boundary line between their two claims and each stayed six months of the year there while the other worked on the Santa Fe Railroad.

They could kill ducks and geese from their kitchen door so they had plenty of fowl for food. Because they had no oil for lamps, they saved the duck tails and burned them at night for a little light.

Mrs. T. R. Cantwell
Sterling, Kan. 67579

Sundial on the Sill

In the second summer at my father's pioneer home, I went to a subscription school. We were taught by an "old maid," who was probably in her twenties. She was holding down a claim while her brother worked with the gang building the railroad across the state.

The brother had taken with him their only timepiece. Our teacher told time by the position of the sun which came in the windows of the half dugout. The sills were marked like a sundial. As the days lengthened, the shadow moved past the marks on the sills, leaving us without an accurate "clock." Small matter. There was little need for close scheduling in those days.

Anna Holmes
Donna, Texas 78537

Stones for Warmth

In the cold Kansas winter Grandfather set the box of his covered wagon down in the ground and some of the children slept in it, with hot stones and buffalo robes to keep them warm.

Mrs. Maud Beattie
Inman, Kan. 67546

Not a Drop To Waste

Water! How precious it was! We never wasted it in those days on our claim in southern Colorado near Trinidad. Those who had it in springs or wells on their claims shared it with those who did not, and how desirable and valuable a claim was could often be determined by the availability of water for drinking, washing, and watering livestock.

When our neighbors found a spring running from the side of a hill on their claim, they dug a hole and made a concrete basin to catch the water. And they put in a pipe outlet.

We would load two barrels in our wagon and drive 10 miles to the spring. We ran the wagon under the pipe and let the water fall into the barrels. We kept the barrels in the shade at our homestead, and the supply would last about two weeks.

In winter we melted snow. At least we did not have to make the long trip in cold weather.

Mrs. Elva Tyler
Costa Mesa, Calif. 92627

Solar Cooling

Ninety years ago, on a farm in Iowa, my grandparents used the sun to keep foods cool.

On a hot day, Grandmother would partially fill a tub of water and in the center she would put a crock or vessel of some kind containing the milk, butter, or other foods she wished to "refrigerate." She would place a lid on the crock, then cover it with a piece of blanket, making sure the edges fell into the water. The cover was doused well with water and the blanket was re-wet frequently. In a few hours, the contents of the crock would be cool as a result of the sun's evaporation of the water.

Mary Margaret Thompson
624 Southwest Tenth Street
Oklahoma City, Okla. 73125

Wet-sand Cooler

Water was plentiful in the sand hills of Yuma County, Colorado, where my father homesteaded, and we did not have to go deep to find a good supply. We had a big 50-gallon wood barrel buried in the ground, and we kept the sand around the barrel damp so that milk and butter we held in the barrel would be cool.

Altho water was plentiful in the ground, it was scarce for deer and other animals. Coyotes and jackrabbits thrived; there were lots of them.

Mabel G. Riddle
Box 124
Reynolds, Neb. 68429

Milk Cache Under the Floor

When Mother had no place to keep milk cool on our homestead in Custer County, Oklahoma, she dug a hole in the floor of the dugout under the dining table. It was big enough to hold three one-gallon crocks. She put milk in the jars, laid plates over the top, and covered them with a wet cloth. Then she put a board over the hole so we would not kick dirt into it while we were eating at the table.

She declared the milk kept about as well there as it did in the refrigerator she used in later years.

T. C. Stanley
503 Wainwright
Elk City, Okla. 73644

Blessed By the Chimney

My paternal grandparents came to Colorado over a hundred years ago. My father, whose birthday was September 7, 1860, was the first white child born in Colorado Territory.

The family were strict Presbyterians and breaking the Sabbath was a deadly sin. So it was a shameful day indeed when their nearest neighbor, from five miles away, came by and found them building a chimney for their fireplace. You see, it was Sunday.

In recalling the incident years later, Grandma said, "It was my fault. I was supposed to keep track of the days, but somehow I must have missed one. I confessed to God and asked him to forgive me, and I'm sure he did. You know, that was the best drawing chimney we ever had!"

Georgia L. Pinkerton
15380 Chelsea Drive
Cambrian Park, Calif. 95154

He Bobbed the Fence

One bleak winter when fuel and food were scarce on our west Kansas homestead, Father and Mother pined for the good old days back East, remembering among other things that wood, especially hedge wood, was often wasted there. Here on the treeless plains, there wasn't a stick for kindling. Paper was scarce, coal oil had to be saved for lamps, and it took a genius to start a fire with "prairie coal."

Then Father had an idea. He decided the long sturdy hedge

posts he had brought from back East and used to fence the pasture and yard were maybe a little taller than necessary. He sawed the top from each post and made a nice pile of wood to ease Mother's nostalgia.

Mrs. Louise Brumfield
Jetmore, Kan. 67854

Coal Was for Company

Most of the fuel we burned in the early 1900s came from our pasture in Holt County, Nebraska. But we did have coal. It was kept covered with sand to prevent "slacking" by exposure to air. We dug some out on special occasions when we wanted to show off for company.

Carl W. Moss
2112 Harlan Street
Denver, Colo. 80214

Steam Heat

My oldest brother was born in January on my parents' dugout along the Little Blue River. It was a severe winter with much snow, and the only fuel the family had was wet cornstalks. They filled the oven with wet stalks and piled them on the stove top to dry. Imagine how little heat they must have had!

Mother said she had only two diapers for her first baby. Each time he was changed she would wash the diaper. All water came from melted snow.

Mrs. Lillie Johnson
205 E. Holland
Minden, Neb. 68959

Drive Provided Fuel

Children in the Nathan Beecham family, living near Liberal, Kan., in the 1880s, had a singular duty. They watched for cattle drives as the herds were moved north to the railroad line at Dodge City, and they remembered where the cattle had been bedded down for the night.

In a few days after the herd had moved on, the family would drive to the bedding ground and collect cow chips there.

The trick was to "harvest" after the chips were dried and before other settlers had spotted the good supply.

Elsie M. Davison
7701 DeVore Drive
Newman Hall
Oklahoma City, Okla. 73132

Hot Wood From Section 37

Wood was scarce on the open prairie of early Iowa, and land speculators would buy the timber lands along the rivers so sodbusters would have no source of wood to burn. When the settlers couldn't get fuel for winter, they would have to sell their farms cheap.

Many of the speculators lived out of state, so local men would go to Rock Creek, on the border between Floyd and Mitchel counties, and cut wood. If they were caught, they claimed they were cutting wood on Section 37—but there are only 36 sections in a township.

One such speculator hired a horse and a cutter to inspect his property in the dead of winter. He was hailed by a man with a team and wagon, who needed help with logs too heavy for one man to lift. The next spring when the owner checked the surveyor's stakes, he found he had helped load his own logs.

The corner schoolhouse was often heated with wood from Section 37.

The main wood on the prairie was hazel brush and water willows, neither large enough for fuel.

One winter at Bishop Knoll, a farm which has been in my family since 1874, the cattle shed was brought into the house for fuel, a couple of boards at a time.

Around 1900 many windbreaks of pine and cottonwood were planted, and willow, a fast-growing tree, often was included in the breaks as a source of fuel.

Robert Bishop
Nora Springs, Iowa 50458

A Useful Weed

We pioneer people called the prairie yucca "soapweed." I was grown before I knew soapweed was not a word found in a dictionary.

Fuel was scarce on the treeless prairie. On the flats and rolling range country, "prairie coal" kept the houses warm and the food cooking, but in the sandhills country, where the soapweed was a pest and had to be dug out before the plow could do much good, it was often used for fuel.

We sometimes visited friends on a homestead close to the sandhills where we saw huge stacks of soapweed piled for winter fuel. They had a drum-type heater which they could stoke with whole soapweed. What a roaring fire those weeds could make!

I remember being there for dinner when the hostess cut slices of bread from huge loaves she had baked in an outdoor oven. It was made of sod and plastered on the outside. On bake days soapweeds were burned in the oven, then the glowing ashes were raked even, and the big pans of bread placed on the hot ashes.

We from the "prairie coal" area almost envied these folks who had clean fuel that burned like oil and perfumed their yard with a kind of prairie fragrance.

Mrs. Louise Brumfield
Jetmore, Kan. 67854

Warnings and News Came by Phone

One of the most interesting items in our Holt County, Nebraska, homestead was a crank telephone mounted on the wall in the dining room. Dangling from the bottom was a plug which

Mother used to connect a line running east to Amelia and Chambers to a second line running south, eventually reaching Burwell. A series of rings brought Mother to the phone where she joined the lines so a caller on one system could converse with a person on the other.

That phone system was something! The line ran on fence posts until it came to a gate; then it was overpassed by tall uprights to permit hayracks to enter and leave the field without interrupting the phone service.

After a blizzard we could follow the telephone wire and pick up prairie chickens that had flown against it and died. We hung them, frozen, until we wanted to eat them.

This was a mutually owned system, and each homesteader maintained the line across his land. Sometimes the wire would break, and the owner would patrol his section, find the break, and repair it in his own fashion. Many times the line was broken in several places between our telephone and "central," but eventually service would be restored.

A signal of short rings would summon all subscribers for an important announcement. Special calls were put thru for prairie fire warnings and national news items. I remember when the news of the assassination of President McKinley came in 1901, my father called us together for family prayer.

> Carl W. Moss
> Denver, Colo. 80214

She Earned a New Well

My mother remembers those early days (1903) when she and my father came west and settled in Oklahoma Territory. For about 18 months they hauled water, traveling five miles over a bumpy trail to and from a well on another farm. Families for miles around came to the well, and as many as six wagons might be gathered there at one time. Each family would wait patiently for its turn, or help others hand-pump a supply for drinking, washing, and watering livestock.

My mother taught school to buy steel well casing when a new well was built on the homeplace. After she earned a diploma at Teachers Normal, Woodward, in the summer session, most schools had signed teachers. So she took her horse, and riding sidesaddle, crossed the country until she found a school 18 miles away. Her salary was $30 a month for teaching 33 students in all grades for the three-month term. She worked mornings, nights, and weekends for her board and room.

In the spring of 1905 my parents were able to buy 210 feet of well casing. The well was put down to a depth of 207 feet with a posthole digger and a sand bucket. When the digger was full, a horse pulled the dirt out. My mother led the horse while my daddy emptied the bucket and started it back down the hole.

When my parents finished their well, they shared the water with neighbors until finances permitted them to dig their own wells.

Ruby Wieden
Route 1, Box 35
Arnett, Okla. 73832

Deep Freezer

On my husband's claim in Bacca County, Colorado, where I went as a bride in 1917, we had no water and we had to haul it three miles, sometimes five miles, in large barrels. My husband tried to dig a well, but the water was so deep and the rock so thick, he had to give it up.

But he did make use of the unfinished well. He placed a large pole across the opening some feet below the rim and there he hung jackrabbits, cottontails, wild ducks—anything he had shot —and let them freeze. He put a heavy cover over the well and weighted it down.

Outside the east window of our half dugout, he built a box about the size of the lower sash. Two ends of the box were screened, and the side attached to the window frame was open. We put what we wanted to keep cool into the box, and I was able to raise the window sash and reach the food from inside the house.

The crib for our baby was a 100-pound Arbuckle coffee box, well padded.

Ruth Curt Fields
307 South Divison, #21
Auburn, Wash. 98002

Raising Water Was a Gentle Art

On that 160-acre claim my father had near Wild Horse, Colo., where we lived between 1910 and 1913, we had a circular well, hand dug. We pulled water out with a bucket that was lowered to water level on a rope. It was important to swing the bucket carefully so it would tip enough to let the water run into it. When it was full, the bucket was lifted slowly and carried carefully to the house so that not a precious drop would spill.

Maude Nelson Hoblyn
Route 1, Box 53
Mason City, Neb. 68855

News Traveled on Barbed Wire

Within five years after we moved to a 160-acre place in Morton County, Kansas, there were probably a dozen homes widely scattered in our area and the people there decided to set up a phone system.

Each family was responsible for its own phone, so we all installed a phone box on the wall and provided the two dry-cell batteries which powered it. Turning a crank on the box would ring every telephone on the line; each family had its own signal, such as two shorts, or a short and a long, and so forth.

The telephone line was the top wire of barbed wire fence, which gave good service only if all splices were tight. If there was a gate in the fence, a pole or a two-by-four about 10 feet high was nailed to each gate post, and then a wire was wrapped tightly around the fence wire and run to the top of one high pole, fastened to an insulator there, strung across the opening to the insulator on the second pole and down to the fence line again. Stringing wire in this manner permitted high loads to pass thru the gate.

These phones saved the people many trips, but reception was not always good and in times of high wind it could be poor.

Floyd Morgan
Route 2, Box 266
Vashon, Wash. 98070

Candle Lanterns

My grandfather, R. S. Kirkpatrick, often wished he had kept one of the little lanterns made of perforated tin that held a candle. They didn't give much light, but they kept the candle flame from going out in the wind.

He remembered the lanterns which were used the night his brother was lost.

The boy had gone to bring in the cattle one evening, riding his pony along a nearby "crick." When he did not return at darkness, the family, alarmed, began a search. Neighbors were notified and they came from the scattered farms adjoining my great-grandparents' homestead. As they entered the house, each man placed his lantern on the porch, and there they sat in a row, barely able to dispel the gloom of night.

The boy was found, but he had been injured. He was not able to tell clearly what had happened to him in the dark pastures. His mother taught him to walk again and how to eat, as if he were a baby once more. He never regained full intelligence altho he lived for many years.

The symbol of the little lanterns was one that stayed in Grandfather's memory as long as he told stories of his early Iowa boyhood.

Mrs. Omar J. Stoutner
Keota, Iowa 52248

Multi-party Line

William Craig had lived 10 years on his ranch on Florida Mesa, near Durango, Colo., when he decided in 1908 that he should have a telephone. He obtained permission to build a line westward from his home to a point where he could tap the Farmington, Colo. line.

This was the first and for some time the only telephone on the Mesa and it soon became community property. Anyone needing phone service headed for the Craig house. There he found a key to the back door. He simply went inside and made his call.

One common purpose of those early calls was to summon the doctor for confinement cases.

Carrie Craig Dyer
925 Third Avenue
Durango, Colo. 81301

CHAPTER 4: Wind and Weather

Buried in Snow

Early settlers in Harrison County, Iowa, built their barns and houses in the timber and used the open prairie for grazing. There were reasons: Altho the soil was very rich in the timber, settlers had to clear the ground before it could be planted, a task which required much time and labor. And they liked the shelter of the woods in the terrible winters.

One of the coldest winters occurred in 1856 when a blizzard, thought to be the worst storm in over 100 years, buried all the buildings one settler had erected on the open prairie. He was able to dig himself out of his house and work his way to the barn where he cut a hole in the roof so he could water his stock.

My great-grandfather, a boy at the time, said the snow reached five feet in the timber and the drifts were much higher on the open ground. Caught with insufficient fuel, his family cut down a nearby tree and drug it to the house for burning.

Ruth Divelbess Crispin
Wichita, Kan. 67220

The Biggest, Blackest Cloud!

Solomon Smith and his wife, Sophia, arriving in Kansas in 1872, stopped in Salina, a 14-year-old hamlet with about 1,200 persons. The Smiths rented a little board shanty there for $20 a month.

One day Solomon walked out to look at land, so different from that in his native Maryland. Returning home that evening, he saw rolling in from the southwest the biggest, blackest cloud he had ever seen. Never had he viewed a cloud like that one; he knew the end was at hand!

He raced home, demanding that the trunks be brought out and packed for immediate flight. He was leaving for Maryland.

Sophia remained calm. "No," was her response.

And so Solomon Smith sat out his first Kansas tornado. He frequently gave credit to Sophia for having greater courage than he did.

—Rewritten from an article in the *Salina Advertiser-Sun,* submitted by Solomon Smith's great-granddaughter.

Mrs. Herman L. Dingler
Enterprise, Kan. 67441

A Nebraska Sandstorm

When we were advised to take our ailing little daughter west and to live outside as much as possible, my husband went to North Platte, Neb. by train and filed on the last piece of land left for homesteading in McPherson County under the Kinkaid Act. He didn't even look at the land.

At home again he made an overshot box to set on the double box of the wagon, and he added bows and covered them with canvas. Our bed slats and spring were laid on the overshot box and topped with a tick of shucks and a featherbed. Trunks and boxes went under the bed, with a folding table, some chairs, a kerosene stove, pots and pans, a lantern, soap and towels and a washbasin.

Southeast of North Platte, we drove into a sandstorm. Taking the canvas cover off the bows, we lashed it tightly over our bed and cooking equipment. We tied towels across our faces because the sand cut and stung. Blown full of sand—our clothes were packed—we were so heavy we could hardly get down from the wagon.

Right then I didn't think much of the West.

In McPherson County, our new home, we didn't care for the wide open spaces all covered with bunch grass, soapweeds and rattlesnakes. And we didn't like the fleas, the little black bugs that could jump and bite. They were everywhere.

We stayed on that claim, built a house, and raised crops of potatoes, beans, and corn, and one day we were able to make a trip to North Platte to prove up on our homestead.

Mrs. Carl E. Feikert
519 West Eighteenth Street
Kearney, Neb. 68847

Storm Was Too Much for Tent Home

We unloaded on a piece of ground where nothing but tall grass was growing when we arrived at our homestead in Wallace County, Kansas. My father, mother and oldest brother put up a tent which was to be a temporary home for the seven of us.

Lacking any other fuel, Father gathered cow chips for cooking our first meal.

In the night it stormed and snowed. Our tent fell down. Altho Father fixed it, he knew we couldn't stay there. He walked several miles to a house, and the people there asked Mother and my baby brother and me (I was eight) to stay with them. They came for us in a wagon and we waited in their home two days for the storm to pass. My father and other brothers stayed with a man who lived by himself. When the weather was clear we went back to the tent.

A small house, a single room only 6 by 6 feet, was finished in April, and we lived there thru the summer, until we had a larger sod house.

Another brother, who came when I was 10 years old, was born in the time of a storm. Father sent one of the older boys to a neighbor's house to ask for help, and the woman there walked two-and-a-half miles to come to us. She did the work of a nurse and a doctor, with my father's help. I was called to get up in the night to find clothes for the new baby.

Alice Hale
Route 4, Box 120-A
Seymour, Mo. 65746

Flood Followed Him

My great-uncle had a house on low land near the Kansas River at Lawrence. Every time the river left its banks he was flooded out. Many times he lost heavily as crops were washed out and his house damaged. So one year when the river threatened, he carried all the furniture and household possessions to a cabin on higher ground which had never been touched by flood waters.

But this time the river cut a new channel; it washed away the cabin, the furniture—everything.

The house beside the river stayed safe and dry.

E. F. Stepanek
Cuba, Kan. 66940

Beans Were the Days' Menu

On that eastern Colorado homestead, we lived on the prairie surrounded by grass, sagebrush and soapweeds. Our home was a one-room shack covered with tar paper, and we had a barn, and a chicken house made of wire and straw. We also had a windmill which my dad climbed to turn the blades so we could have fresh water when the wind didn't blow.

When we went anywhere it was by wagon or on horseback. To visit my grandparents, who lived a couple of miles away, my mother rode a horse with me and my brother behind her and my baby sister in front.

One day in winter we were helping my dad gather cow chips when our neighbor came by and stopped to help us. It was cloudy and stormy. He told us to put all our bedding, food and anything that would freeze in the wagon and come to his house because a bad storm was coming. His house was a dugout built in a bank—and warm.

It snowed so much the men had to tunnel thru it to the barn to care for the animals and milk the cows. We were eating beans, mostly, for days before the men could get to town for supplies—a trip which took them a couple of days.

Had we stayed in our tar-paper shack we would have frozen!

Mrs. Luretta Fay Cline
16669 D Street
Victorville, Calif. 92392

Deep Snow in the Pass

My brother-in-law and his wife were traveling with us when we took out for Price Creek, Colo., my husband having found a better place to farm there. Our belongings had been shipped earlier by train, but my brother-in-law had a cow and a calf to trail.

Within five miles of our new home, a storm hit, and we had to camp for three days in our wagons. When the weather cleared the snow was about three feet deep in the pass we had yet to cross.

The men emptied what they could from the wagons and doubled up the teams to get them to the top of the rise. Taking turns carrying my four-month-old baby and pushing or carrying the calf, we waded those five miles in waist-deep snow.

We stopped at the first house we saw, and the people there gave us warm clothing and dried ours in the oven.

The men didn't get in for seven more hours.

Mrs. Ethel McAlary Lasater
Myrtle Creek, Ore. 97457

No Chimney Meant No Fire

I homesteaded a claim in Butte County, South Dakota. What a life—hot summer, cold winter!

I had only a laundry stove with a draw on the pipe for cooking and baking. The chimney was a stove pipe put out the side of the house. For fuel, I went for miles, picking up chips in gunny sacks and dragging them home.

In the winter of 1911-12, my chimney blew away in a blizzard. I couldn't have a bit of fire; it was so cold! I got down on my knees and prayed.

I decided I must walk to a neighbor's house a mile-and-a-half away. I put on all the coats I owned, and wrapped my apron around my cat so it wouldn't freeze. I also had a white Spitz dog, and I said to him, "We are going to Mary's. Lead us to Mary." There was only a trail to follow and the snow was two feet deep and still falling.

When we reached a creek, I hollered to my neighbor for help. She brought a rope and threw it across the creek. When I had tied it around my waist, she pulled me over the creek where the snow was over my head. I was nearly frozen when I reached her place.

I stayed there three days before I could go for help to fix my chimney.

Mrs. Bertha Hamblin Adams
Maple Heights Nursing Home
Mapleton, Iowa 51034

Lost in a Blizzard

This story dates back to the early '80s when my father was homesteading in the north central part of the Dakota Territory. He lived alone for eight or nine years before he married. As often as he could, he visited relatives in the Red River Valley. Usually he made the journey in one day with his driving horse, Bronco Bill, hitched to a buggy in summer and to a cutter in winter.

One winter morning after visiting relatives, he left for home. It clouded up and began to snow; in the afternoon the wind came up, and soon a blizzard raged. When darkness set in, Father had no idea where he was. He held the reins, and Bill trudged into the storm. The going was slow.

Snowbanks from previous snows that winter were huge and

solid, and Old Bill was walking on one when he stopped suddenly. Father noticed a scraping sound under the cutter and got out to see what was wrong. Then he heard a dog bark and saw a glimmer of light, and a man was hollering "Who's up there?"

It was the familiar voice of a homesteader who lived four miles from Father's claim. The joy of those men was indescribable as they worked to get horse and cutter down from the roof. The snow had drifted up to the low slanting roof of the shack and Old Bill had found his way to safe refuge.

Mrs. P. F. Rosproy
Route 1, Box 44
Spearville, Kan. 67876

A Wyoming Winter To Remember

In the spring of 1910 my dad took up a homestead 10 miles south of Upton, Wyo. It is the winter of that year I want to write about.

I guess you could say winter started August 28. Dad went to town that morning in his shirt sleeves and had to borrow a fur coat from the livery man to wear home. The storm was so bad he couldn't see the road, so he gave the horses their head and let them find the way. Usually a trip to town meant Dad would be home at 5:30 in the afternoon, but he didn't arrive until after 9 o'clock and was nearly frozen for he had been on the road since about 2 o'clock.

We had quite a bit of nice weather after that first blizzard, but when winter really set in, it brought hardships such as we had never seen before. Many horses and cattle died because the deep snows made it impossible to get feed to them.

The spring that supplied our water was snowed under, so Dad put a large barrel in the kitchen to hold water. We kept a wash boiler filled with snow on the stove. As the snow melted we poured the water in the barrel and refilled the boiler with snow.

New Year's Eve was so nice we went to a neighbor's home to watch the new year in. Shortly after we arrived there the snow started. Dad managed to make it home the second day of the storm, but Mother, Sister, and I stayed until the third day when the wind blew itself out.

While we were away from home, the fire went out and our winter supply of potatoes froze. We couldn't afford to waste them, so we ate frozen spuds for a long time.

We had quite a few sage hens, jack rabbits, and cottontails to eat that winter. To relieve the monotony of fried rabbit, we ground the meat and made rabbitburgers.

Dorothy Hiers
733 Mynster, Apt. 2
Council Bluffs, Iowa 51501

Wind Delayed the Search

I remember the blizzard of '84-'85. Mother came to Kansas in the early '80s, and homesteaded a claim just over the line in Stafford County. We were living in a sod house there the year of the storm.

My brother was caught at one of our neighbor's and his friends would not let him start for home for fear he would be lost in the snow.

Mother grew uneasy about him. Wrapping a quilt around herself, she walked across the prairie to the neighbor's house to find him. Sometimes the wind was so strong that she was forced to sit down, huddled in her quilt, until it eased and she could go on. She traveled a mile in that storm and brought my brother safely back with her to our home.

Mother worked for other families in the country and often rode a roan pony to work. At one place she helped with the butchering and was given some meat. On the way home wolves, attracted by the smell of fresh meat, followed her. She held on to the meat and arrived at the soddy unharmed.

The claim Mother had is covered with oil wells today.

Charles Stephenson
Columbia, Mo. 65201

No Fit Night!

One night in northern Nebraska, when a blizzard was raging, my husband's grandmother, Sarah Mead, opened the door, closed it quickly, and reached for her apron to wipe the snow from her face, saying "Only coyotes and Methodist preachers would be out on a night like this!"

Her grandson, my husband, served 41 years as a Methodist minister in Colorado, Montana and Nebraska, and he can vouch that he was out in many storms and a few blizzards.

Alice Foster
1810 King Street
Sidney, Neb. 69162

A Wind-propelled Apron

At our homestead in Stanley County, South Dakota, where we moved in 1910, the sun shone every day and the wind blew every day.

When Mother and we younger children were walking on the prairie one day, we noticed Mother's apron was missing. It had come untied and had blown away unnoticed by any of us. In a letter back to Iowa, Mother mentioned the loss to her sister.

Her sister wrote back that something with a tail passed over Iowa. She had called it Haley's Comet, but it probably was Mother's apron.

Mrs. Fred C. Nelson
Route 2
Lucas, Iowa 50151

Hens Survived in Their Dugout

On a beautiful spring day in early March, 1910, my mother and her three children and my aunt with two children arrived by train at Sligo, Colo., 50 miles southeast of Cheyenne, Wyo., to be met by my father and uncle who took us to our homestead site 10 miles farther east.

The men had preceded us in February, by emigrant boxcar, bringing all our possessions to this new land. They had erected a floorless barn to shelter us until our houses could be built.

Before the month was out, we were engulfed in a blizzard. The men, fearing the roof of the barn would be blown away, climbed the wall to fasten wires to the rafters and tie them to the anchor posts. For several days, it was unsafe to venture more than a few feet from the shelter of the barn.

It was impossible for my uncle to find his way thru the storm to the dugout where he had housed his small flock of Buff Orpington hens. On the third day, to his surprise, he found them very much alive, altho the canvas roof, under the weight of the heavy snow, had caved in on them.

Our team of horses was safely sheltered in a lean-to hastily constructed by the men at the onset of the storm.

During the blizzard, two teen-age boys were frozen to death when they became lost trying to find their way to a neighbor who lived only a quarter of a mile away from their camp.

Ruby Bigelow
Route 3, Box 3600
Grandview, Wash. 98930

The Well Served as a Storm Refuge

I was born in 1900, the year a hurricane killed so many people in Galveston, Texas. The tail of the storm dumped heavy rain in western Oklahoma where my parents were living. A gopher hole in the top of the dugout let water pour in on me, a little baby lying in bed. The top of the dugout caved in and my mother rescued me just in time to save my life.

When I was eight, my mother died, and my brothers and I went to live with our grandparents. I was there on April 27, 1912, when a cyclone swept across the farm and tore up all the buildings except the rock house we lived in. It broke all but one window in the house and it jammed the doors shut so tight that we could not open them and had to crawl out a window.

My uncle and aunt had a new house on the same farm. They saw the cyclone coming toward them and started to run across the road to a neighbor's cellar. When they realized they could not get there in time, they got down in an old dug well. The cyclone went over them and destroyed their house. So much rain fell that the old well was nearly full of water when they climbed out of it.

Some of our neighbors lost their houses, too, and one woman lost her home and 80 handpieced quilts. At one house, the cyclone blew away the walls but left the floor with the rug, organ and organ stool standing in place.

When my uncle rebuilt his house, he put in a cellar with a door at each end.

Mrs. J. O. Kidling
Route 2
Foss, Okla. 73647

CHAPTER 5: Homestead Homemaking

Flowers on the Roof

Great-grandmother was furious when her husband chose a spot near the creek for their dugout, their first home in 1893 on a claim in western Oklahoma. She complained because the dugout was out of sight of the section line and "you can't see folks go by." He argued for the convenience of water and won.

To this home Great-grandmother brought flower seeds, tamaracks, and a canary. The flowers were planted on the roof of the dugout. A snake found and swallowed the canary, but with the bird inside him, he couldn't escape from the bird cage and he was doomed.

Florence Alkire
Seiling, Okla. 73663

A Cup of Burley for Breakfast?

Our sod house in our early days in Colorado had deep windows. Mother stored utensils and staple foods at one end of a windowsill near the stove, while Dad kept his tobacco in a coffee tin at the opposite end of the sill.

On one particular winter morning, he opened his tobacco tin. "Where in thunder is my tobacco?" he growled.

"Heaven sakes!" Mother gasped, as a nose-tingling odor

wafted up from the coffeepot. "I made coffee out of your tobacco!" For years, Dad told the story of Mother's peculiar way of making coffee, but at the time he didn't think it funny. He was "tobacco broke" and the store where he could buy a new supply was nine miles away at Arena, Colo.

Irene Jackson
Kit Carson, Colo. 80825

Made at Home

My grandparents came from White County, Tennessee, to Texas County, Missouri, in 1871. Grandfather built a log cabin with a fireplace where Grandmother cooked their meals for 14 years. Grandfather made the furniture—beds, table, chairs, cupboards, wardrobe for clothing, and a stand table which I still have.

They raised sheep, sheared them, picked burrs and trash from the wool, washed it, carded it, spun it, and wove it into cloth for clothing and blankets. They raised cotton and flax to make into cloth. Grandmother did lots of knitting for her family, making socks, mittens, and sweaters.

The big peach and apple orchard yielded quantities of fruit, much of which Grandmother dried. Fruit sold at 10 cents a bushel, pick-it-yourself.

For light the family first used a saucer of grease with a twisted rag for a wick. Then came candles, homemade, and then a brass lamp that burned kerosene.

I still wonder how they did so much work.

Mrs. Chester Jones
Houston, Mo. 65483

Quail Made a Tasty Dish

The winter Papa had to spend several weeks in a hospital in Kansas City, Mama kept us five children back home on a farm in Mitchell County, Kansas. To help keep things going, each of us children was assigned a job.

Our uncle made a trap he called a "Figure 4" so Bub and I—we were about six and eight years old—could catch quail. It was a box of wood and wire in which we hung a head of kaffir corn. When a bird entered to eat the corn, he tripped a board that closed the opening.

It was our job to check the Figure 4's each day, keep the traps baited, and bring home any birds we had caught. We did very well, for I remember the family table was often graced with tasty dishes Mama made from quail. Once we even caught a prairie chicken.

Gracia M. Webb
Alton, Kan. 67623

Bitter Cure

Mother made our cold medicine, boiling together onions, catnip and horehound and sweetening it with sorghum or honey. It was bitter medicine, but good for a cold.

Mrs. Anna Atkinson
Longton, Kan. 67352

Dog-power Churned the Butter

As a boy I did many a churning with barrel churns. They came in different sizes—5, 10 and 15 gallons. On each side of the wooden churn were two metal spindles that fitted in the top of a U-shaped frame. One spindle was squared on the end to take a crank or pulley—a crank if powered by hand, the pulley if powered by animal.

At the bottom was a plug to drain off the buttermilk after the butter had gathered. The lid fastened with three clamps. A peep hole in the lid was fitted with a glass about the size of a nickle so the operator could see when churning was done; the glass would become clear. The churn was also equipped with a small petcock to relieve pressure during churning.

The treadmill had two rollers spaced three to four feet apart with a pulley on the end of one roller. One roller was about a foot lower than the other. The floor of the chute, which was large enough to accommodate a big dog or a goat, was a continuous belt which ran over the rollers. The harnessed dog or goat was led into the chute, and as the animal pulled, the pressure of its feet on the belt caused it to move the pulley, creating the necessary power to turn the churn.

Tom Oldham
Orleans, Neb. 68966

Shoo, Shoo, Fly!

Remember fly time on the prairie? My grandmother did and told these tales:

The children had to swish the flies off the cows at milking time with leafy branches. At the table, a youngster stood at each end with a branch to chase the flies away. It wasn't uncommon to hear Mother say, "Be more careful—you just knocked a fly in his coffee! Here, let me skim it out for you."

After dinner, it was, "You girls do up the dishes quick, before they call more flies." Then she would take a bottle of sorghum and make a thin line on the table; with a quick swoop of her hand she would catch a bunch of flies at their sticky roost, lift the lip of the cookstove, and drop them in.

One of the first niceties for prairie dining was a little screen that fit over each dish and was removed as a person served himself, then was replaced before the dish was passed on.

Robert Bishop
Nora Springs, Iowa 50458

The Fruits of Her Labor Lost

Minor diseases could be as shattering as major ones for the pioneer family. My mother tells of such a disaster which occurred one year while she and nine brothers and sisters were living at home on a sandy farm in northwest Oklahoma.

Grandmother prepared her winter's store of jam and jellies from wild plums and grapes. Her supply represented hours of work in preparing the fruit, and boiling the juice and sugar on a wood range when temperatures often passed the 100 degree mark. And tho the fruit was hers for the picking, purchase of the sugar was made with hard-earned money.

Grandmother stored the jams and jellies on shelves in a cellar.

Heavy rains came that year, drenching the dirt walls of the cellar and soaking the floor. The walls caved in, the shelves collapsed, and the jars fell and broke. The fruits of her labor were lost.

Grandmother, ill from the shock, took to her bed for several days. And her family ate sparingly of jam and jelly that winter.

Florence Alkire
Seiling, Okla. 73663

Loving Care Was the Best Medicine

In the country where I lived many, many years ago, store-bought medicines were scarce. Our illnesses were treated with homemade remedies. Only during the most severe illnesses, after loving home care had failed, was the doctor summoned. Someone had to ride 10 miles on horseback to tell him he was needed.

At our house a bottle of "spirits," or homemade whiskey, was marked "Medicine only" and kept on the highest shelf. At the onset of a cold, Mama mixed a hot toddy and made us drink it while she greased us with an ointment she compounded of lard and pine rosin. Then she firmly fastened a wool flannel around the chest and dressed us for bed. And there we stayed until all signs of the "grippe" had vanished.

When I was in the first grade, my older sisters said that some kids at school had the itch. "We'll be disgraced," they declared, "if we catch it. If you ever itch, don't dare to scratch and don't tell a soul except Mama."

So one day in the middle of winter when the teacher looked at my hands and asked about the bumps on my neck, I replied "They're chigger bites." Teacher whispered, "It's the itch."

Mama felt a child with the itch was a disgrace, a sign she had failed to teach her daughters cleanliness. With much embarrassment she consulted Dad about a treatment. He was our stepfather, much older than Mama, and he was knowledgeable about many things. He told her to dig and boil the roots of pokeweed and bathe my sisters and me in the brew. She cooked a huge potful, poured the solution into a tub, plunged us into it and scrubbed us. It burned and we were screaming and yelling with pain! Finally Dad came to the door and said, "I didn't aim for you to skin them alive. I meant for you to put it on with a cotton dabber." Mother then doused us with cold water and covered us liberally with fresh unsalted butter.

The itch mites were gone but it took many days for our skin to heal despite Mama's frequent applications of fresh sweet cream and butter. We held our heads high and marched to school, knowing we were once again in good standing. We blamed our reddened skin on cold weather and chapping.

We were often warned not to fondle the barn cats, but sometimes I couldn't resist playing with the kittens. When I came up with ringworm, Mama sent me to the walnut pile to find a soft-hulled nut with juice in it. This she rubbed over the ringworm until it disappeared.

One time I sat down in a patch of greenery that looked cool and inviting at the end of the cotton row. A few days later I was covered with huge clear blisters. Dad cut some gunshells apart and shook out the powder into a bowl of sweet cream. He said it was the only thing to cure poison oak, that being the name of the pretty leaves I had rested on.

When we were scratched by barbed wire or stepped on a rusty nail, we soaked the injury in coal oil for hours, or else "You'll have lockjaw and die." I grew up more afraid of lockjaw than any other thing. I sat for hours soaking my rusty wounds and hating the smell of coal oil.

After the summer's end, Mama always gathered the grainy

seed of the Jerusalem oak which she boiled with sorghum to make a brittle candy patty. When she decided we kids needed worming, we ate the candy for three days as a special treat. She also mixed some with the feed she threw out for the chickens.

I often wondered how Mama knew when I was worried or could not sleep. At those times she gave me a glass of warm milk with a teaspoon of honey and a dash of nutmeg. Then she would sit beside the bed and encourage me to talk while she held my hand or massaged my back. The combination of the drink and her companionship caused my restlessness to vanish, and I often fell asleep before finishing my talk.

Home remedies and closeness went together in those days. Closeness may have been one of the best remedies we had.

> Viola O. Griffis
> Route 7, Box 39
> Joplin, Mo. 64801

Shag Rug

One late fall a family from New York state arrived in Kansas and joined a settlement. The only place they could find to live was an abandoned dugout. Here they spent the winter in comfort.

Toward spring the housewife decided the family should clean house—at least remove the top dirt from the floor. To her surprise she discovered a reason for the warmth afforded by the dugout. Buffalo hides, she found, had been pegged hair-side-up to the dirt floor.

> Mrs. Edgar L. Williams
> Rural Route 3
> Norton, Kan. 67654

The Down-home Breakfast Specials

In those old days, when we butchered, we would fry the meat and put it in stone jars, pouring grease over it. Sausage was made into patties, fried, and stored in crocks filled with lard.

Mama put up tomatoes, cooking them in a kettle and then pouring them into half-gallon sirup pails. She sealed the lids down with sealing wax.

Here are some of the breakfast menus we liked: Hot baking powder biscuits and milk gravy; buckwheat pancakes made with yeast and set overnight, with sausages; homemade bread toasted in the oven, spread with homemade butter and liberally sprinkled with sugar, with coffee and cream poured over all. For that last dish, only homemade bread would do. Good!

Mrs. Moody Messick
1501 Alston
Marysville, Kan. 66508

Grandma's Home Doctoring

Colds, burns, earaches—we had them all when we lived on that Colorado homestead. Grandma often treated our ailments.

For chest colds, the cure was skunk grease. Grandma fried the fat of skunks my uncle hunted and skinned, and she rubbed the stuff generously on the chest and topped it with a warm flannel cloth.

Sometimes the treatment was a mustard plaster. More than once a bit of my skin came off with the plaster.

For coughs, we took a teaspoon of kerosene and sugar.

Flaxseed poultices were used for infections and slivers in the hands.

A hot baked potato was cut open and placed over my aching ear. I lay on it and let the steam help relieve the pain.

When my uncle burned his arm, a friend walked more than a mile for cattails so Grandma could mix them with lard and spread over the burn. When the arm healed, there wasn't a scar.

Every spring we were given molasses and sulfur to clear the blood—whatever that means. I can't even eat molasses cookies today.

Alice Foster
Sidney, Neb. 69162

Adventure in Canning

My mother was born in 1861, the year the War Between the States began, and she told me many stories of the past.

Her father was very progressive. He bought the first wood cookstove in this part of the country, Springfield, Mo. He and Grandmother were the first in the community to can foods in glass jars.

They were afraid of the jars breaking in the house, so they built a fire outside and cooked apples. Then with the jar in a pan of hot water, they filled it and screwed on the lid. Neighbors from far and wide came to watch. The apples kept.

Mrs. P. M. Dickens
Route 1, Box 676-B
Springfield, Mo. 65803

A Word to the Cook

The sod house my father built on his Oklahoma claim leaked—as most sod houses did. My mother told of a big rain which came thru the roof as if it were a sieve. She was making biscuits at the time! Grandma gave her this advice: "Turn that dishpan on your head and keep the mud off the biscuits."

Mrs. Roy Curry
Enid, Okla. 73701

Carpet on the Floor

My brother and his bride, and I, a single woman, had adjoining homesteads near Stanton, Kan. Our shacks were part dugouts, with dirt floors and dirt walls to ground level. My shack had a floor covered with a layer of cane topped with a rag carpet. The furniture was a bunk bed, a homemade table, crates for cupboards, a small cook stove, and a couple of old chairs.

I taught school nearby and pulled broom corn and cut milo maize with a small knife to earn money which enabled me to pay out on the land after living there two years.

65

Sometimes church was held in the schoolhouse. Some of the sermons were in German, which we didn't understand, but we enjoyed singing and meeting our neighbors.

Mrs. Mary Heiland
Bucklin, Kan. 67834

Cured in Troublesome Creek

Grandfather knew how to make many things the pioneers used. His specialties were doubletrees, singletrees and neck yokes from wood of the hackberry and red elm trees. After they were shaped and planed, he fastened them to a log and laid them in the rushing waters of Troublesome Creek to cure.

When seasoned, these woods turned reddish brown and became as hard as flint. It took a steel bit to cut the holes for the fittings.

Ethel Scar
Earlham, Iowa 50072

Coffee Dregs for Floor Care

When Great Aunt Sophyia was left a widow with three small children, a sister persuaded her to come West and homestead a government claim.

Neighbors came for miles with teams and plows and they broke the sod and built her a two-room shack. The house had a dirt floor.

Aunt Sophyia was neat and clean. She washed her hands a dozen times while preparing a meal, "for fear of getting dirt in the vituals," she would say. But she had one bad habit. Every morning she would empty the dregs from her coffee cup on the floor. "After all," she would say, "it is a dirt floor and I always dampen it with water before I sweep, so what difference does it make?"

Her family and friends in the city had begged her for years to come home for a visit. She was homesick, so she decided to go. What do you think happened the very first morning she was there? Horror of horrors! Without thinking, she flipped the dregs from her coffee cup on her friend's beautifully waxed kitchen floor!

Mrs. R. D. Cole
Box 160
Meade, Kan. 67864

Cracklin' Soap

We four sisters helped make everything we ate or used on the farm. Our hardest job was making soap.

Dad would build a big hopper which we filled with ashes from our wood fires. To wet down the ashes, we had to carry water half a mile. The water ran thru the hopper, and what dripped into a pan was lye.

We put the lye in a big pot over a fire, with cracklings or any kind of grease, and boiled it until it thickened.

Brother, a little of that soap would go a long way! We were always treating our hands because it ate the skin off.

Myra Poston
Dill City, Okla. 73641

Homemade Medicines

Doctors were few when settlers moved into new territories and Great-grandmother was often called on to diagnose common ailments and prescribe medicines for their treatment. She depended on the healthful properties of native plants and herbs.

Many older citizens remember the sulfur and molasses prescribed as an annual spring tonic; it was supposed to thin the blood and improve one's physical condition for spring work. Roots of the sassafras tree were a popular blood thinner, too.

Children were taught to gather leaves from the pokeberry, curly dock, dandelion and wild mustard. The spring greens, when cooked, added variety to dull meals and supposedly improved digestion.

For treating food poisoning and stomach disorders, Great-grandmother might recommend a beverage made from bergamot, fennel, catnip, peppermint, ginger or yarrow leaves. Her medicine for relieving rheumatic pains was a tea brewed from the leaves of the cinquefoil. To stop a nosebleed, she applied crushed leaves of the yarrow. Bee stings were treated with white ash leaves, while chewing the prickly ash berry soothed toothaches.

Skin tonics utilized the bark of the white oak or the dogwood and geranium roots. Some of these ingredients are still listed on the labels of medicine bottles.

After paying a bill for miracle drugs today, one almost longs for the potent all-curing tonics from Great-grandmother's kitchen.

Vera M. Brooks
Marysville, Kan. 66508

Imported Salads

Grandma loved greens, and when she moved from an eastern home, fearing the barren plains would lack materials for her spring "salads," she brought along seeds of lamb's-quarters and dandelion.

I remember her yard in Nebraska, well-seeded with dandelions. Grandma always had healthful spring greens right at her door.

Mrs. Levi Gingrich
LaVerne, Calif. 91750

A Bed of Beans

Dry beans had a large place in our diet during our early homestead days on the northeastern plains of Colorado. I recall saying to an old bachelor who stopped by in the summer of 1910, "In Iowa, we used this ladle to skim milk, but now we dip bean soup with it."

Pinto beans produced well until the soil became too badly eroded. The year of the most abundant harvest there was no market for beans and we had no dry storage place. Some boards were used to partition off a bin in the family living room.

When friends from Iowa came for a visit, my mother and brother relinquished their beds to the company and made beds for themselves on the beans.

Those beans were eventually sold for $15 a ton.

Ruby Bigelow
Route 3, Box 3600
Grandview, Wash. 98930

Pumpkin Rings

The lovely prairie autumn was going swiftly by. The cottonwood trees had changed from their rich green leaves to that autumn yellow, unique to cottonwoods, and all of a sudden they stood naked, their leaves swirling on the ground.

Winter was coming to Baca County, Colorado, where my father and mother, Alfred and Eva Meltabarger, had claimed land in 1913 and where they raised 12 children.

Cucumbers in a five-gallon jar of salt brine, strong enough to float an egg, would make delicious pickles for jaded appetites thru the winter. Beets sat red in jars ready for a Sunday dinner. Only two green rows, the upper leaves nipped by frost, showed where plump carrots and fat turnips were waiting their turns to take the monotony from winter meals.

The shuck beans and dried corn hung in sacks in the back room. The corn had been cut from the cob in the roasting-ear state and spread thinly on clean flour sacks to dry on top of the shed. A sheet was stretched over the grain, a large rock on each corner holding it taunt and making a little tent to keep out dust and insects. Every hour or so, my sisters and I were given big spoons and sent to the shed roof to lift the sheet and stir the corn; this continued until it was perfectly dry.

Now it was time to dry pumpkin rings. Earlier my brothers had hauled the pumpkins to a bin where the broomcorn seed was stored, in a rock building where they wouldn't freeze. I lifted the pumpkins from the box, handing them to my sisters. The firm ones were put in tubs for Mother at the house; the ones "going soft" were stacked for my brothers to take to the hogs. We girls broke a couple open for the chickens to pick.

In our dugout, Mother sliced the pumpkins in thin rings. I was big enough to peel the rings without breaking them; my sister Wanda cut the pulp from the inside; and sister Iva cubed rings accidentally broken too badly to hang on the wire. The broken pieces were put to cook; they would be made into butter or pies.

A single slash thru the ring let us hang the pumpkin on a wire stretched behind the kitchen stove. A towel was spread over the rings and they were left there until they were dry.

The dried pumpkin went into sacks to join the corn and beans in the back room.

Thru the winter the rings were broken into pieces to be soaked overnight and cooked for butter or pies. Dried pumpkin had a slightly different taste from fresh pumpkin, but it certainly did brighten our winter and early spring meals.

Evallee Myers Forpahl
481 West Sixth Avenue
Springfield, Colo. 81073

CHAPTER 6: Critters and Crawlin' Things

Johnny Appleseed's Crop Saved the Baby

The apples that year were big and red when Great-grandmother gathered them in the orchard near her new log cabin in northeastern Kentucky, an orchard which had been planted by Johnny Appleseed.

Her husband was in the woods cutting logs and she was sewing strips of handwoven woolen together for a blanket. The baby slept in the cradle. Because the fall day was sunny and warm, the door was open. Suddenly a shadow crossed the doorway, followed by a huge bear. In terror, Granny watched as he went toward the baby.

She had heard bears were fond of ripe apples, so she grabbed some and offered them to the bear just as he picked up the baby. He dropped the baby in the cradle and reached for the apples as Granny threw them out the door. When the bear lunged after the apples, Granny yanked the heavy timber door shut and bolted it. The bear ate the apples and tried to come back into the cabin, but was barred by the door.

Granny was still shaking when her husband returned and pounded on the door which she had been afraid to open.

Mrs. Gayle Killinger
420 Mississippi Street
Lawrence, Kan. 66044

Baby Stolen by Bear

My brother-in-law tells this story, passed down from his great-grandfather:

He and his wife were laboring together on their homestead, and of course, their baby son was taken to the field, to be wrapped in a blanket and laid nearby.

Once, to their horror, they glanced up to see a huge bear carrying off their precious bundle. The father followed. The bear stopped, lowered the baby to the ground, and covered it until only a mound of leaves showed. Then the bear left.

The father snatched the child and put the leaves back in place. He then hid to see what would happen.

The bear came back with two cubs. She went at once to the pile of leaves and threw herself down upon it. She dug around, but her warm live prey was gone.

You can bet that father and mother thanked God for protecting their treasure from death.

> Thelma Blosser Loucks
> Route 1
> Box 143
> Canton, Kan. 67428

He Carried His Cap

It happened in central Missouri over a hundred years ago, and my grandfather told the story this way:

"I had heard the grown folks say that they were scared until their hair stood straight up on their head, but I never believed it!

"Late one afternoon, my pa sent me, a boy of about six, to my uncle's house, a short walk thru the woods, to borrow an iron wedge. He said I could play with my cousin until bedtime, which in those days, was very early. I stayed a good while and it was dark when I started home.

"I called my dogs, but they were playing, too, and were slow in coming. When I heard the leaves behind me rustle, I turned to wait for my pet hound. And my heart just sort of stopped. It seemed jammed into my body where it had no business being. The animal was not my hound, but a large gray wolf. The wolf stood motionless, I stood motionless. When the leaves rustled again, I thought I would be faced with a pack of wolves—and me with no weapon but a big iron wedge. But there stood my dogs! The wolf trotted away.

"The rest of the way home I carried the wedge in one hand and my cap in the other. The cap wouldn't stay on my head. My hair kept pushing it off!"

Marjorie Z. Dawson
Leavenworth, Kan. 66048

Ingenious Egg Hoist

When my husband's grandparents homesteaded in Kansas, they built a small three-room house with a small upstairs. At the bottom of the stairway was a small landing and there they kept their eggs in a box.

One night Grandma was awakened by a noise. Bump! bump! bump! it went. She thought it was a loose board hitting the house, blown by the wind. Several nights later she was awakened again by the same sound. She woke her husband who got a lamp and tried to locate the noise.

It seemed to come from the stairwell, so Granddad opened the door carefully. What do you think he saw?

A rat lying on his back was holding an egg on his belly with his feet, and another rat was pulling him up the stairs by the tail.

The next morning Grandma went upstairs to see if she could find where the rats were putting the eggs. Behind a trunk she found more than 50 eggs, not one of them broken. She also found a bushel basket of empty eggshells.

Mrs. Audrey Troester
1221 Main
Parsons, Kan. 67357

He Refused To Be Cat Food

My great-grandfather, he claimed, was afraid of no man or beast—except a panther. If a panther could tear up and destroy a choice team, he asked, what in the world would it do to a man?

One time during his travels he took time out to try for a deer. Since deer hunting requires great patience and quiet, he lay face down beside a log near a run. He fell asleep and woke to discover he was being covered with leaves by a panther which probably thought he was dead. He lay very quiet for fear the panther would discover his find was still alive. When the panther had him well hidden, the animal sauntered off to scream for his mate.

Great-grandfather lit out. From a safe distance, he looked back to see the two panthers spring on the pile of leaves and begin tearing it apart.

If Great-grandfather had been there, he could never have told me this tale.

Doris Virginia Reed
Washburn, Mo. 65772

Gray Mares Made a Pious Team

My husband's grandparents, Port and Emma Sproul, were early day settlers near Baileyville, Kan. (then called Haytown because of the large amount of hay shipped from that station).

They liked the land around Baileyville for homesteading and bought 80 acres at, I believe, a price of $5 an acre. I have heard Grandma (Emma) say many times that when they got to Baileyville they had nowhere to tie the horses except to the wheels of their wagon. That was in the spring of 1880.

Grandpa loved his horses and kept fine mares for raising colts. We have been told he averaged four colts a year for 36 years. He particularly loved a 4-horse team of gray mares. Two of these pulled the spring wagon used as a hearse for the first five funerals in the community. The first five who died were all under 30 years of age.

74

When the hearse reached the grave, the lines were removed from the team and used to lower the casket into the grave. The gray mares stood with heads lowered and one knee bent until the lines were put back. What we thought might be just a family story was confirmed by a man we didn't know. He said he didn't know how anyone could have such a pious team and that he had never seen a team so well trained.

Mrs. Albert S. Hay, Jr.
Onaga, Kan. 66521

Dog Swam the Wide Missouri

A good dog was a treasure for the pioneer family. Coming from Iowa to Nebraska, my father's family had their dog, Lion, with them. At the Iowa border, there was a toll for crossing the river. The attendant asked a dollar for the dog, knowing few could leave an animal behind.

Grandfather whispered to Grandmother, "We can't afford to pay that much!" At the same time he grabbed Lion by the back of the neck and threw him into the water. My father's heart stood still for he loved that dog.

But Lion, a large black dog, beat them to the other side and was standing on the bank shaking himself when the family arrived in Nebraska.

Mrs. Irvin Anderson
Stromsburg, Neb. 68666

The Horsenappers

Father had only recently completed our soddy on his claim in southwest Nebraska in the year 1885 when his team of mules and his neighbor's team of horses disappeared one night. The animals had been staked out so they could graze, and they had got loose or were stolen.

We searched all around for them. Father even borrowed a horse from a cowboy and rode for three days looking for them, but to no avail. Then Father and his neighbor posted a reward of $5 for their return. That evening some cowboys brought them in.

We learned later that the cowboys had hidden the horses and mules in a canyon about two miles away and waited for a reward to be offered.

Arthur Parsons
Pawnee Rock, Kan. 67567

Horses Walked the Planks

When Canada proved too cold for my parents, they were determined to return to Goodland, Kan., where they had lived previously. For the trip they bought a pair of western horses, small, strong and surefooted.

On the route they came to a long railroad trestle which spanned a ravine. Only by crossing the trestle could they continue on the road.

Using ties which he found at the side of the tracks, my father began to lay them between the ties which supported the rails.

A man passing along the road suggested another arrangement. "Make a single line of ties," he said. "Then take your lead horse by the bridle and lead it down that line of ties. See what the other horse does when you start."

Papa made a long line of ties as the man advised. Then he unhitched the horses, and taking the bridle of one horse, he started to walk the trestle on that narrow row of ties. The horse put his nose between Papa's shoulders and followed; the second horse put his nose on the first one's rump, at the root of the tail, and they walked quietly across the trestle. The men pulled the wagon across.

Mrs. Nora Schesser
8008 Blind Pass Rd.
St. Petersburg, Fla. 33706

Oh! His Aching Head!

Aunt Ret had a dog that would bring in any cow Aunt told him to. He often came in with a swollen head, the result of an

76

encounter with a snake. He would lie on a platform outside the door and Aunt would prepare a poultice of homemade soap and sugar or milk and bread, and she would wrap his head in it. When the poultice was dry, he'd peel it off and be ready for another snake.

Lula Husband Bright
Route 1, Box 8
North Platte, Neb. 69101

Terror at the Tailgate

When a freight contractor, working out of Arkansas City, Kan., could not make a haul himself, he hired a man to accompany his eleven-year-old son into Oklahoma with the loaded wagon and mule teams.

Having delivered the freight, the pair were on the return trip. One nightfall found them near a small stream with dense thickets along the banks. About half a mile back, a homesteader had invited them to camp in his yard, but this location by the stream seemed ideal, with water and wild grass for the two teams of mules.

Soon coffee was boiling and the man and boy were eating fried potatoes, bacon, and beans. The mules were staked out and a full moon was rising in the east. All gave promise of a peaceful restful night as the pair bedded down in the empty freight wagon and fell into sound sleep.

The boy never knew what brought him wide awake; perhaps it was the soft thud of a body landing or the frightened squeal of a mule. Sitting bolt upright in bed, the man and boy saw, sitting on the tailgate of the wagon and clearly outlined against the full moon, a huge panther, one of the most feared animals in the territory. Many tales were told of their attacking man and all those tales came flooding back.

The animal sat looking at them a few moments—an eternity to the boy—then jumped from the wagon and sped away.

Quickly, the travelers untied the mules, hitched up the wagon, and drove to the higher safer ground of the homesteader's yard.

It was a night that eleven-year-old would recall the rest of his life.

Mrs. Austin Young
1602 Manfield
Winfield, Kan. 67156

A Bear Scare

For a trip from Canada to Kansas, my parents bought a covered wagon and camping equipment. When they stopped for the night, they slept in the wagon. Often after they had gone to bed, they would hear bears close by, looking for table scraps.

One night Papa decided to go out and scare the bear away. The bear turned on him, and Papa whirled and came dashing back to the wagon. As frightened as she was, my mother had to laugh. She said he looked so comical in his voluminous nightshirt, halfway between his knees and feet, and flapping.

The bear was permitted to finish his meal in peace.

Mrs. Nora Schesser
8008 Blind Pass Rd.
St. Petersburg, Fla. 33706

The Collie Saved the Corn

This story about a collie dog took place on our several hundred acre farm where I was born in 1882. The place was known as the Yakle Estate and was located near Louden City, Ill., which is now called Old Post Oak.

The inland highway to St. Louis passed our farm, and covered wagons came by daily, usually going west. Down the road a piece we had a wooded area where the travelers would stop for the night. My father gave them permission to water their horses and to carry buckets of water to their camp sites. He offered fruits and vegetables to families who wanted them, and even milk for the small children. Some wagons had "Missouri or Bust" blazened on their white canvas sides; they might have coops of chickens wired to the end gates, and sometimes cows were tied there, too.

One morning in early spring, after several of the wagons had moved on, we heard a scratching at the back door and there we found a footsore young collie dog. He was a pathetic sight, with paws worn so raw from the endless miles of travel that he could barely stand.

My father showed my brother and me how to fashion boots from the leather tops of Mother's worn-out buttoned shoes. We smeared tallow on the dog's feet to soothe his wounds, then we tied on the boots. At first he would try to work the boots off, but I patiently put them back again until he seemed to sense that I was trying to help, and he let them alone.

When his feet were well, he followed me everywhere. He even slept beneath my window.

One night in late fall, after the crops were harvested but before the rains came, he really repaid us for our kindness to him.

To the east of the house, about a quarter mile away, was an area covered with a thick growth of white oaks, intertwined with hazelnut bushes, sumac, and berry vines. It was a fire hazard, to be sure. It bordered on a 60-acre field of corn, which had been harvested only the day before this incident occurred. The corn shocks were left leaning against the fence line, and the field had been planted in winter wheat.

I was awakened that night by the dog which was barking and racing back and forth from my window to the front of the house. I ran to the front door and opened it. The collie bounded in and ran to my parent's room, still barking. My father knew something was wrong for the dog was usually quiet. He called my brothers, and they came tumbling down the stairs, dressing as they ran, and shouting that from their window they could see fire in the timber near the cornfield.

With a team of horses, my father and brothers worked the rest of the night to move all the corn shocks to the middle of the seeded wheat field and run a drag around the fence line. The crop was saved.

Spring came, and we watched a few wagons come from the west. Their owners had given up and were going back to their former homes. The signs on their wagons were altered to read "Busted."

In early summer we had some such wagons in our grove for the night. When the men came to the well for water, the collie leaped for joy. His master had come back. My father tried to buy the dog, offering the man much needed supplies. He would not sell.

In the morning the wagons left and so did the collie. He did not even say goodbye. I cried over the loss of my companion. Actually he had thanked us in many ways for his keep, particularly in saving 60 acres of corn.

Mrs. Luella R. Morris
Box 9250 Westhill Road
Lakeside, Calif. 92040

Pig in the Well

When we settled on a homestead in Oklahoma, we hauled water from the Canadian River, three miles away, until a well was dug on the home place. A well was a novelty to me, a nine-year-old girl, and I loved to look down at the water. Altho I had been warned to keep the cover in place, sometimes I would lift the lid and steal a peek.

One day when I was watering pigs, I decided to look down into the well. As soon as I lifted the lid, a little pig fell in.

My first impulse was not to tell, but when I realized the pig would drown and spoil the water, I ran for my mother. We hurried to rescue the pig.

She lowered me into the well, riding on a bucket tied to a rope. The water was only shoulder deep, so I could stand on the bottom to pick up the pig. Time after time he climbed out of the bucket. I took off my hood and put it around him, tying the strings to the bucket bail, and Mama pulled him up. Then she lowered the bucket again to lift me out of the well.

I had been a disobedient child, but somehow I never was punished for lifting the lid and almost drowning a little pig.

Mrs. C. H. Campbell
321 Lincoln
Ordway, Colo. 81063

Critters and Crawlers Gave Her the Creeps

As a bride in June, 1910, I joined my husband who had already spent six months on a homestead in western South Dakota, about 20 miles from Fort Pierre on the Missouri River. Home was a one-room shack, covered with blue building paper inside and black tarpaper outside. All was held in place by nails with shiny, one-inch heads.

We were within sight of one other shack, but there were no homes in the five-mile stretch to the railway station from which we hauled water in two cream cans behind the single seat of our open buggy.

My husband worked at that time in the railway mail service, a job which kept him from home two nights in succession. We would drive together to the depot; he would board the mail car and I, with my full water cans, would drive home alone.

The trail led thru prairie dog town, an area much burrowed by the little animals and much populated by rattlers. Except in cold weather, we never passed thru it without seeing from one to four snakes. Indeed, this was rattlesnake country. During that summer, three were killed on our immediate grounds. Whenever I entered our cave, I was aware of the possibility of meeting one. I never swung my feet out of bed without first peering under it for snakes.

One dampish morning, I found numerous inch-long, brown-shelled worms on the floor. I could make no impression on them except by cracking their crusts with a hammer. More were falling on the linoleum. I looked up to see hundreds clinging to the ceiling and walls. I covered the water pail and my hair, and spent the forenoon sweeping them from the walls and out the open

81

doorway. I never knew what they were or where they came from.

One night I was roused from sleep by a peculiar noise and a trembling house. I realized that I probably had forgotten to close the barbed-wire gate, and that our half-acre enclosure had been invaded by range cattle. One of them, having a good shoulder-rub on a corner of the house, was shivering the shack's framework. I couldn't have them horning holes thru our paper walls or breaking the cave's roof; I had to get up and get them out! Moving seven or eight perverse critters thru an obscure opening in a fence was a most frustrating chore. The task took a long time, and our buggy whip was given a good workout.

Despite critters, crawlers, creeps, and sub-zero cold in a paper house, we completed the required 14 months of living on the place. With the payment of 50 cents an acre, my husband "proved up" on his claim. It was a rough quarter section fit only for grazing. Even so, the profits from the property helped him to a start in the newspaper field. And the whole experience was one we should not want to have missed.

Grace C. Robinson
1728 Simoloa Avenue
Pasadena, Calif. 91104

A Snitching Snake

This incident happened in June, 1912, when I was visiting my parents on a homestead in the dryland country of northern Colorado.

One beautiful warm morning Mother and I stopped our work for a snack. We gave my two-and-a-half-year-old daughter a piece of bread spread with fresh butter, and she went outside and sat down in her little chair to eat it.

Mother and I were visiting when we heard the baby scream. I rushed outside in time to see a large spotted snake crawling away with the bread in its mouth.

As soon as she saw me, the child stopped crying and said, "The mouse took my bread!"

She had scratches on her hand from playing with a kitten, and I was sure the snake had bitten her. After some fearful moments we realized she had not been hurt.

We were told later that the snake that stole the bread probably was a milk snake attracted by the fresh butter.

Mrs. I. H. Drennon
1136 La Porte
Fort Collins, Colo. 80521

Wolves, Keep Your Distance!

My folks homesteaded in Montana in the early 1900s. When we needed groceries during the winter, my father would cull out some chickens and take them to town to sell for groceries.

My mother and brother and I were watching him one time when he was about a mile from home. What looked like several calves were following him at a distance of about 100 yards.

When he returned Mother asked whose calves they were.

"They weren't calves," he said. "They were timber wolves. And if they had come too close, I was ready to turn the chickens loose."

From then on he carried a shotgun when he went to town.

Preston Bryson
Route 2
Beatrice, Neb. 68310

Horses in Disguise

Horse thieves were as common as coyotes in central Kansas when my parents lived there in a dugout. My father had an especially fine horse called Bim, which he had trained so that no one except my father could catch him. For safety, Bim was turned out to pasture every night.

One night when my parents were returning from a dance, they saw two men on horses down the road. As they came closer they could see one horse wearing a cloth with holes cut out to look like spots, and the second horse was covered with a dark cloth. Were these men horse thieves? Had they caught Bim?

When they arrived home, a whistle brought Bim to the barn. He was safe.

But the next day a neighbor came for help. He had lost his last two horses.

Bim was never stolen altho several times thieves tried to catch him.

Mrs. A. K. Ingham
Beverly, Kan. 67423

My Pals Had Four Feet

When I was a child on a homestead in southern Colorado, I had no children to play with, yet I had many friends.

There was Smokey, a horse that fiddled with my hair and never moved a foot when I played under him; Bonnie, a dog that hunted and killed snakes and guarded me from inquisitive range cattle; and Old Annie, a goat that was mean to most people but loved me and stood patiently lending the support I needed after a serious illness. And there was Annie's kid; he played tag with me in the yard and see-sawed with delight on a board which my father placed over a sawhorse for us.

Pauline Sasse Wallis
Lecoma Star Route
Rolla, Mo. 65401

Pig Price Too High!

As a gift to my sister June, our uncle in Iowa sent two young Duroc bred sows. They started us in the hog business on the farm near Elmwood, Okla., which Papa had bought as a relinquishment in 1907.

Papa raised lots of maize and kaffir corn as grain for the hogs and they bought many things needed for the farm.

I remember the day June sold a pig to a neighbor lady for five dollars. When Papa came home, he was horrified that she had charged such a price, and he sent her to return three dollars to the buyer.

Fern Pounds
Elmwood, Okla. 73935

CHAPTER 7: Neighbors Good and Bad

Builders in a Free State

My grandfather, N. W. Murphy, left his trade as a carpenter, sold his farms, built his covered wagon and left Fort Madison, Iowa, in 1860. He came to Kansas to help make it a free state—or so he told his wife.

With daughters, 12 and eight years old, and a son, two, the Murphys spent the first winter at Shawnee Mission with the Indians. Grandmother, formerly a schoolteacher, helped with the teaching. The little girls, who attended the school, had time off when the Indians went on the warpath.

In the spring the family purchased land from the Indians in Johnson County, west of the Missouri border. The Indians were friends and neighbors.

Having completed his house, Grandfather next built a log cabin schoolhouse, declaring he would not have his children grow up in a land without schools. His wife's maiden sister came to be the teacher.

Then the Murphys said there must be a worship service, and they held the first church service in the township in their house. A circuit rider came from Lawrence, riding a pony and carrying in his saddlebags a change of clothing and any donations that were given for his services.

As soon as he had chosen his land, Grandfather started an

orchard. Grandmother laid out her garden, planting sage and herbs brought from Iowa. The herbs grown there produced many of the ingredients for her tonics and salves.

The daughters of the family often told how long were the days. They dipped candles; dried apples, corn and pumpkin; knitted mittens, stockings and caps; made lye and soap; sewed all the clothing; quilted and tacked bedding; and cooked endlessly. The Murphys fed anyone who came to the place. Grandmother thought she kept the Indians happy by giving them doughnuts.

Often they kept people who were traveling on the Underground Railroad. When Grandmother would hear that they had arrived in Baldwin, Kan., she would remark, "Thank God, that many more souls are saved."

The son loved the Indians; they taught him to ride their ponies and to shoot their bows and arrows.

When Grandfather made a trip back to Iowa to collect money due him, his wife was left with three children on the prairie. She kept plenty of doughnuts on hand for Indians. Sometimes they would stretch out in front of her fireplace and nap.

Grandfather returned bringing money for the family, maple sugar and other gifts from relatives, and coal oil lamps because "They would help so much for the church service."

Ever the organizer, Grandfather deeded an acre of his farm to establish a burying ground. He reserved a strip thru the middle, the length of the acre, for the use of his family. When a second son was born to the family and died within a few months, the child was the first to be buried there. Five generations rest there now.

Grandfather often made coffins for families in the community; Grandmother lined them with whatever materials were at hand.

Social life centered in the church, school and the Grange. Programs were apt to be temperance lectures or debates concerned with a leading issue of the day. In the home the social events were quilting parties, comfort tackings, husking bees and taffy pulls, the taffy cooked with home-produced sorghum.

In 1865 a church was built in the township; the Murphys were charter members of the congregation.

As more settlers came to the prairie, Grandmother would say, "It is so good, in the morning, to see the smoke from some neighbor's cabin." To her that meant they were establishing a community.

Mrs. Thelma Murphy Quaintance
Olathe, Kan. 66061

We Needed Each Other

The homestead my father bought in the Missouri Ozarks had only a two-room log cabin chinked with mud. We carried water in buckets from two large springs quite a distance from the house, and we did our washing at a stock pond, with washtubs, a washboard and a large iron kettle for heating water. After the clothes were washed, we hung them on bushes. How sweet they smelled drying in the sunshine!

My father hauled lumber for a sawmill 15 miles away and built a four-room house. Until it was finished, several of the children slept in a grape arbor near the log house.

I helped my mother rive board for shingles on our house. A tree was cut down and logs sawed. We drove wedges in the end of the log to split it.

With my sister I hauled rock in our brother's wagon and built a quarter mile of rock fence. We tried to dig a well and we dug until it was so deep we could no longer throw out the dirt. Father hired two men to finish it.

Mother made jams and jellies from grapes and plums. We also picked blackberries and wild grapes, and Mother canned them in tins which were sealed with wax melted in a ladle and poured around the lid.

We helped our neighbors strip sorghum cane and took molasses in return. Navy beans, black-eyed peas and cowpeas were picked on shares. We raised a garden. Corn was cut from the cob and dried, and apples, peaches and pears were also dried. At the approach of winter a large hole was dug in a corner of the garden, lined with straw and filled with potatoes, cabbage, squash, turnips and apples. A covering of straw and dirt kept them from freezing.

We had very little money in those first homestead days. But we had courage and love and the will to fight want and earn our keep. We needed a home, food and each other, and God made it possible for us to have all of them.

Mrs. Mae Miller
Tarzana, Calif. 91356

Kindnesses Repaid

When Grandfather was away at war and my grandmother lived with her children in western Missouri in the 1860s, an old Indian chief would come to her door to ask for flour or cornmeal. Grandmother always gave it to him.

The day the rumor spread that Indians would burn the town and the nearby houses, the old Indian brought horses and took my grandmother and her children to his camp. He let them stay there until the scare was over.

Mrs. Hazel Bacon Dern
Route 2, Box 39
Hope, Ark. 71801

When Uncle Louie Shot an Outlaw

Great-uncle Louie always took his rifle with him when he rode out on horseback. One day when he was riding along the Kansas River west of Lawrence, a short distance from his home, a shot was fired at him. He raised his rifle and returned fire. He suspected he had hit someone, but he did not wait to see. Instead he headed for town to notify the sheriff.

On the road he met a posse and the sheriff riding in search of members of the Jesse James gang who had broken out of jail.

Uncle told the sheriff his story and led him to a little peninsula made by the curve of the river where the exchange of shots had taken place.

The sheriff was unbelieving when Louie told him he had wounded a man.

"Louie," he said, "you could never hit a man at that distance. I could go over there and stand by that log and let you shoot at me all day, and you'd never hit me."

The sheriff's posse rode to the peninsula and there they found the cornered fugitives. One of them had been shot.

"When you decide to take a shot at me, Louie," the sheriff remarked when the outlaws had been captured, "let me know ahead of time so I can leave the country."

People in the community laughed about this incident for a long time.

E. F. Stepanek
Cuba, Kan. 66940

Times Were Hard on Children

We came to Colorado, my mother and six children, to homestead in southeastern Colorado, eight miles northeast of the Two Buttes mountains.

We had lots of good neighbors. Our fun centered at the schoolhouse where we had spelling bees, ciphering matches, literary meetings, card games, ball games, and, of course, dances. My oldest brother played the violin, and my younger brother and I played the guitar and organ.

Funerals were held in the schoolhouse, too. Many children died. I remember a 12-year-old boy who died of a ruptured appendix, a 10-year-old girl who died after being bitten by a rattlesnake, and a two-year-old child who died of summer complaint.

The men would all come to dig the grave, and our minister would preach the funeral service.

My mother gave five acres of land for a cemetery where many of the old homesteaders are buried.

Mrs. Louella Canfield Perkins
Lamar, Colo. 81052

90

The Disappearing House

A family from Iowa came to Stanley County, South Dakota, in the fall of 1910 to homestead on a tract adjoining our land. They stayed at our home the first night. Upon their arrival we pointed out to them a shack close by our house which they had purchased and planned to live in.

The next morning we noticed the man walking up a little hill and looking around. When he came to breakfast, he remarked that he could not see his shack from our door, but Mother assured him it was plainly visible. When we went outside to point it out again, there was no shack in sight.

After breakfast the new homesteader walked to the former site of the shack and found tracks to indicate it had been loaded and hauled away during the night. The tracks led to a neighbor's barnyard, and there on a flat rock sat the little shack.

The "new owner" declared it was his property, and no one would go to identify it as belonging to the newcomer. The thief was reputed to have killed a couple of men and everyone was afraid of him.

The new family had to buy another house to live in.

Mrs. Fred C. Nelson
Route 2
Lucas, Iowa 50151

The Neighbors Shared

We came to western Kansas in 1908. That was some time after the Indian troubles had been resolved; however, we suffered many of the privations our earlier relatives had experienced.

My husband filed on a quarter section of school land, and later we bought a relinquishment on another quarter section from a neighbor who went back East.

After filing on the land, Maurice built a little shack there, 16 by 16 feet. We arrived at the shack after dark, and immediately my husband set out to fetch our personal belongings and horses from the old home. All that first night there seemed to be something around the shack, and when daylight came I saw cattle everywhere on the wide prairie surrounding us. I stayed in that shack, with two babies, for a month before my husband returned.

Nearly all the other settlers were young with small families. They were friendly and welcomed strangers. We made our own amusement, mostly with literary and church gatherings. Everyone traveled in wagons to these events, wrapped in plenty of covers so one did not get cold.

In the winter of 1911-12 we could not get to town for supplies for nearly three months. The storm came in December and the snow stayed on the ground until April. Many cattle were lost.

People shared what they had. One of our neighbors had a good supply of flour and when we ran out my husband went to his house to borrow some. The man loaded several sacks on the wagon, saying perhaps someone up our way might be in need of flour. That flour was appreciated by others as well as ourselves.

During the winter one family lost a little baby. They buried it in a snow bank until they could get to a cemetery.

One of the worst things we had to contend with was rattlesnakes. Almost everyone could use a gun and kept one handy for shooting snakes.

In the first years about all the fruit we had was wild plums and wild grapes. We did not raise much garden for three years because we had to haul water, sometimes as far as three miles. The land grew melons nicely without water, so most families had watermelons and cantaloupes. We used to make a butter out of pie melons; it wasn't as good as apple butter, but it was tasty.

Mrs. M. E. Shufelberger
1712 Sixth
Dodge City, Kan. 67801

Rock Mailbox Prevented Blow-aways

We moved to my husband's homestead about 30 miles from Gillette, Wyo., immediately after our marriage. Our house was one room, a corner of which I curtained off for my personal dressing room.

We had a cave that served as a storm cellar and as an extra bedroom when we had company—that is, until we killed rattlesnakes there. Then it was abandoned as a sleeping place.

My husband dug a pit in which we kept our butter. For cream in our coffee, we used canned milk. Neighbors said one could tell how long a homesteader lived in a certain place by the size of his pile of empty tin cans in the ditch.

Big ditches came in handy for building barns. They were deep and wide, and all we had to do was put large logs from bank to bank and we had shelter for horses in winter and shade for stock in summer.

Our mail delivery was unique. When one of us went to town he picked up the mail for all the neighbors. He then put it under a rock, each family having its own rock. The rock was necessary because the wind was very strong about every second day.

All the neighbors were friendly and kind. Altho we were not in the Bible Belt, nearly everyone read the Bible and believed in a loving God. Being so dependent on the weather for our crops, we believed that He who ruled the weather would care for His children. It was a happy, sort of democratic life, since all were poor and no one had occasion to look down on his neighbor.

Mrs. John F. Patterson
Rapid City, S.C. 57701

Help With Tight Shoes

My grandparents lived across the road from Jesse James, and I have heard my aunts tell many times how Jesse would come to their house and work the glove-fitting shoes on my mother's feet before they went to a dance.

Jesse lost out to my father who came West, met my mother, and married her.

Mrs. Hazel Bacon Dern
Hope, Ark. 71801

He Married the Girl Next Door

My husband's parents lived on adjoining homesteads in western Oklahoma. The young man had come from Kansas to farm 120 acres, and the young woman had moved with her parents from Illinois. Two years later they were married.

Because the claim did not have much timber, the young couple lived in a mud hut. They started housekeeping with a stove for cooking, a bed, and a wooden table they made. They dug their wells by hand.

Two children were born there; the young mother was attended by a midwife in each case. After the birth of a son, they traded for land in Missouri, in the community where I was growing up. I met my husband when we were first-graders.

Neva Myers
Route 2, Box 64
Hartville, Mo. 65667

Song of the Lark Lingers On

Homesteading in the Montana hills was probably much like homesteading on the plains. We left our home in Iowa for land in southern Montana in the days when neighbors there were far apart and large herds of cattle and wild horses roamed the open range.

My first experience in Montana was sleeping on the ground where bleached bones of animals were nearby and rattlesnakes were not far away. But to this day the meadowlarks sound sweeter to me because of the Montana meadowlarks I heard that evening.

Our social life was limited to visits with neighbors when we could get together. Church services, weddings and funerals were held in town—and that was 40 miles away.

Mrs. O. R. Roberts
P.O. Box 156
Blakesburg, Iowa 52536

All Were Welcome at Terrace Farm

In 1838 my great-grandfather and his brother bought a large tract of land lying between the Rock and the Kishwaukee rivers near Rockford, Ill. In February of the following year, Great-grandfather left his family at the home in Mt. Morris, N.Y., and with two wagons loaded with tools and provisions, started to the new farm, a trip which would take four weeks. He spent the summer putting in crops and arranging a home. In September he returned to New York for his wife and six children.

The family and three other families, who were moving West, traveled by steamer from Buffalo to Chicago, arriving at Chicago on a Sunday morning.

Rain fell all that day, and since the town of Chicago was laid out on low ground, it was terribly muddy. That evening the family, carrying tallow candle lanterns, walked on narrow plank sidewalks to service in a church at the corner of Clark and Washington streets. They all agreed they wouldn't settle in that swampy town for anything anyone could offer them.

The following day they began the three-day journey to Rockford. Because there were no hotels on the way, the travelers slept on the floor of cabins along the way, using their own bedding.

Great-grandfather had chosen land that had a horseshoe-shaped terrace running thru it. He built his house on this high ground and named his place Terrace Farm. The house, with seven rooms, was exceptionally large for those days. There was a cellar under it, too, and it was kept filled with vegetables.

Itinerant preachers made the place a regular stopping point, and worship services were often held in the house on Sunday afternoon or evening.

For two winters children of the neighborhood gathered there for school. Sometimes as many as 25 came.

The settlers wanted their children to have a good education, so several families joined together and started an academy for older students a few miles west of Rockford. Choosing a name for the academy and the town surrounding it was not hard. Since they had come from Mt. Morris, no other name was considered. My grandfather was a pupil there.

Great-grandfather's home was always open to newcomers, and many stayed with him while building a place to live. Those with destinations farther west often stayed overnight. One such family had a sick child, and my great-grandmother insisted they stay until the child was well. The illness turned out to be smallpox and all the family was stricken. To neighbors who scolded Great-grandmother for keeping them, she replied that the Lord would have thought pretty poorly of her had she turned them away.

My grandfather was 13 when the family came to Illinois. He plowed much of the farm, virgin prairie, with a walking plow. Later the land was divided into four or five farms. After my grandfather was married, he bought out the others in the family and he lived on the farm for a long time.

Grandmother was one of the first in the neighborhood to beautify her yard. She planted flowers of all kinds. Of great interest to all who visited her home was a tub she set out under a tree each spring, with goldfish and pond lilies in it. In the fall she put the tub in the cellar to keep over the winter.

Several years my grandfather bought hogs from neighbors and drove them on foot to Chicago. It was a long slow journey. In later years he told us how he would drive the hogs into enclosures beside the hotel (or tavern as it was called then) and for a dollar he would be provided with a bed for the night, breakfast, feed for a team, and free whiskey—which he never drank. The bed would be in a loft where a half dozen men or more would sleep. He put his money in the hotel safe because he never knew what kind of roommates he might have.

One day people of the community saw a heavy cloud of smoke along the eastern horizon. Two or three days later they learned that the town of Chicago had burned. They were sure it would never be rebuilt, for it was such a low, swampy place. How astonished they would be if they could see Chicago today!

Grandfather sold that farm and moved to western Iowa.

During World War I, the land with some adjacent lands, was taken by the government to create Camp Grant.

Mrs. John L. Strosahl
Lime Springs, Iowa 52155

CHAPTER 8: Times Were Hard

Coffee Break

Aunt Lizzie lived thru the early days on a Kansas homestead, enduring the privations common to all. In the years of crop failure and grasshopper plague, it was hard to obtain the plainest food and luxuries such as coffee and sugar were almost unknown. Molasses was used for sweetin', and grain was roasted and boiled as a substitute for coffee.

Aunt Lizzie went to town one day, and having a little cash, she bought a few groceries, including a pound of coffee beans. She anticipated many cups of delightful brew as coffee grounds were saved and used over and over.

She made the trip with a neighbor who lived some miles away. It was dark when they reached the neighbor's home and Aunt Lizzie walked the remaining miles to her home. Arriving at her dugout in the hillside, she was dismayed to find the paper bag containing the coffee had sprung a leak.

As soon as it was light next morning, she retraced her steps, salvaging the previous coffee beans.

"And do you know," she would say, "I don't believe I lost an ounce of 'em. Did that coffee taste good!"

For Aunt Lizzie that had been a serious coffee break.

Mrs. Ross Blake
Oakhill, Kan. 67472

Harvest of Bones

Our 160-acre homestead was 50 miles from Syracuse, Kan. A trip to town and back took four days. Trips to town were weeks, sometimes months, apart.

When Father was planning to go for supplies, we would pick up a wagonload of bones that were scattered over the treeless prairies. In town the bones brought $8 a load.

Father always carried a bedroll and a lunchbox on these trips. But should he have chosen to eat at the hotel in town, he could have had a good meal, family style, for 25 cents. The price of a room for a night at the hotel was 50 cents.

Floyd Morgan
Vashon, Wash. 98070

Diphtheria Was Greatly Feared

Diphtheria was the most dreaded disease of the frontier. Nathan and Mina Beecham lost two children when an epidemic broke out in the community around El Reno, Okla., where they had established a foothold about 1880.

Two-year-old Nita was stricken, and altho the doctor was summoned at once, she died after only three days. Mina dressed her in white; Nate bought a wooden casket. The family chose a site for the grave on the schoolhouse grounds, and neighbors dug the little grave, but the disease was so contagious and so greatly feared that only the family was at graveside for the funeral.

Within a few days a little son died of the same disease and was buried beside his sister. As other children in the neighborhood died of diphtheria or other diseases, they were buried beside the Beecham children, and thus the Beecham cemetery came into being. The pioneer burial ground has been declared a historical site by the state of Oklahoma.

Elsie M. Davison
Newman Hall
Oklahoma City, Okla. 73132

Paper Matches

The hardships brought about by the drouth during the 1890s figured often in tales told by my parents who were homesteaders in Scott County, Kansas.

One spring they planted a large garden which didn't even sprout. Times were so hard that they dug up the bean seeds and cooked them for food.

If they had a corn crop, Mother made hominy, soaking the corn in a washtub with lye water to take the husks off. On one occasion, my brother, a little toddler, tumbled into the tub. It didn't hurt him—or the corn.

I remember helping my grandmother gather cow chips in the pasture for cookstove fuel.

My mother rolled newspapers to make thin, tight "sticks" about 10 inches long, each with a pointed end. These made the matches go further. She would strike a match to light a kerosene lamp and use a paper roll to carry the flame to the stove or to another lamp.

Mrs. H. H. Hare
Anthony, Kan. 67003

Poor People Shared With Poorer People

My folks pioneered for eight years near Belle Plaine in Wisconsin. My father spoke of these years as the best years of his life—simply wasted! Well-meaning friends had urged him to buy a piece of Wisconsin land in wintertime, and when the snows melted away, Father discovered he had bought a rock pile.

After those years of working away from home to earn enough for food and payments on the rock pile, Father decided to quit Wisconsin and go west in search of better land. With his wife and eight sons he left in the spring of 1875. The highlight of the first leg of the journey was the spectacle of the city of Oshkosh in flames. Oshkosh was burning as they drove by.

The Grants, my father's family, settled near Rhodes (then

Edenville), Iowa. Mother afterward told us they were so short of money and food that they surely would have starved if their neighbors, poor people, too, had not sent in a little food. One kind woman sent over a pan of little new potatoes and Mother hid them until dinnertime so they would be a surprise for the children. They ate the potatoes with salt; there was no milk for gravy.

Father heard of a sod-breaking job 10 miles away and altho he was suffering from dysentery and the plow nearly jerked him to death as it dug into the tough-rooted sod, he lived thru the week, eating mostly cornmeal gruel cooked with milk which his boss's wife prepared for him.

When Saturday night came, Father asked for his week's wages, but the farmer said he had no money. Father insisted that he must draw his pay so he could get a few groceries to take home for his wife and children. When the man still refused, Father, sick and desperate, said "You must pay me or else . . ." He got it and walked the 10 miles home carrying groceries in a sack over his shoulder.

The family grew to 10 with the birth of a ninth son and a daughter in Iowa.

The farm Father bought near Edenville was finally paid for, tho it took many years of privation and hard work.

Gertrude Grant Herzog
Casper, Wyo. 82601

A Talent for Make-do's

My mother married at 18, and she and Dad settled on a homestead in Sherman County, Kansas, in 1887. Times were hard, and Dad often left Mother and the children on the claim while he worked away from home.

Mother knew how to make do with what she had. When a hole burned thru her old cookstove, she mixed a little salt and ashes with water and used it for stove cement. Worked, too!

Too hard up to buy coffee? She put a pan of clean rye in the oven until the grains were dark brown, and then boiled them. Not good coffee, of course, but it was a hot drink for a cold morning.

One day Mother sent Dad after the midwife who lived several miles away. He hitched mules to the wagon and set out, leaving Mother alone except for a three-year-old boy. When he returned home, he found that twin boys had been added to the family. Mother was lying in bed with a baby on each side of her and an umbilical cord in each hand.

When the twins were a few months old, Mother built them a wooden cradle from a Lyons coffee box and some pieces of barrel ends.

Viola Coleman
Denver, Colo. 80209

Chips at a Dollar a Load

A farmer, living near my father's homestead in western Kansas at the turn of the century, hired me to pick up cow chips for him. I would hitch the horses to a wagon early in the morning and drive four or five miles to the cattle range. By the time I had filled the wagon with chips, delivered them to the farmer, and returned home, it was late evening. I was paid one dollar for my day's work.

Floyd Morgan
Vashon, Wash. 98070

He Cried Over Spilled Water

Lack of water created hardship on many homesteads. In my parents' home on the Little Blue River melted snow provided water in the winter. In good weather, they hauled water for miles in a barrel.

One harvest after my father had worked in the field all day, he took his sled and horses, and when evening came, went for a barrel of water. As he drove into the yard, the horses made a sharp turn; the barrel upset.

"That's the one time," my mother told us, "that your daddy sat down and cried. He was so tired!"

Mrs. Lillie Johnson
Minden, Neb. 68959

Children Were His Collateral

Father wanted to buy 80 acres of land that belonged to the railroad, so he went to a banker in Sedgwick, Kan., to borrow money.

The banker asked what security my father could offer. Father told him all he had were four children and his two hands. After discussing the request at some length, the banker said he would take a chance.

Father bought the land.

How many bankers would do that nowadays?

John Black
Bentley, Kan. 67106

We Ate Our Crop

Born and raised in the South, I had always desired to own land. So when I learned that it could be acquired in southern Oklahoma just by filing for a homestead, I persuaded my husband to move west.

We filed on a claim that proved to be prairie land, devoid of trees, but covered with buffalo grass that had to be turned over completely before anything could be planted.

We built a dugout with a single glass window, by a creek, and we lived there for 10 years before we could afford anything better.

Our main food was quails and rabbits. We ground rabbit and added to it what little pork we could afford. It was good eating.

After a few years we planted maize and wheat, but the price of wheat was so low that we decided to eat our crop. I cooked the grain until the kernels burst open, then I drained off the water and let the wheat steam. When it was cold I ground it with a food chopper, generally adding hulled peanuts. We ate it with cream and sugar.

After 15 years of that life, I was glad to relinquish my land and return to civilization. All we had to show for our hard work was a secondhand Ford and three lovely children.

Mrs. Fairy Travis
Elkhart, Kan. 67950

Seven Grew Up With the State

Oklahoma was a very new state when my parents decided it would be a good place for their seven children to live and grow up with the country. Having sold many of their belongings and all of the livestock, they placed the $325 realized from the sale in the bottom of the small basket containing diapers for the baby, and we boarded the train for Oklahoma. Before we left, the straw ticks were emptied and washed, and food was prepared to last the family on the trip.

The $325 would have to buy food from March till crops were gathered in the fall, as well as furniture. Father bought a small cookstove, a heater, and three bedsteads. On arriving at our new home, Father located a strawstack so we could fill our ticks. He unpacked his tools and began to build tables and benches from lumber salvaged from an old shed. For cabinet, dresser, and storage, we used the large boxes our bedding and dishes had been shipped in.

We planted a garden early, as we had back home, and it came up beautifully in a warm April. But one night, after dark, a hard wind blew in from the north, and the next day our garden was dead. Our neighbor explained the damage was from a sandstorm, something we had never heard of.

We hurried to plant again, and just as lettuce was ready to eat and the beans were thrifty and nice, all disappeared one night. Dozens of jack rabbits left their calling cards.

Some of our happiest times came with the arrival of boxes of cast-off clothing from our more well-to-do relatives. We wore what fit us and made the other garments over. We never dreamed of feeling sorry for ourselves for we did not realize how dreadfully poor we were.

What we missed most was reading material, and when subscriptions to magazines and papers ran out we could not renew. One Christmas Mother quilted three quilts in exchange for stacks of old issues of McCall's and The Ladies Home Journal. We rejoiced in this gift and did not realize the work that was involved until years later.

If Mother and Father worried when our table held only bread and a huge bowl of gravy, we children never knew it. We were taught to be thankful for what we had.

We, as well as Oklahoma, grew up, knowing much happiness as we gathered around that homemade table. Our only wish is that things might have been easier for our parents.

Mrs. Zella M. Gamble
Route 1, Box 123
Reydon, Okla. 73660

Poor Man's Country

I am 92 years old and have lived most of my life in Kansas, but as a child I spent three years on an Ozark homestead.

When I was about 10 years old, my parents decided to go to southern Missouri. Mother's brother, who had gone down there, said it was a good place for a poor man. Well, I guess it was, for we went down poor and we came back poorer.

We left Kansas in February and were nearly three weeks on the road which was often bad with mud or deep ruts. Sometimes creeks and rivers were high and we would camp and wait two or three days for the stream to run down so we could ford it. We would stop early in the evening near a stream or spring where we could get wood for a fire and water. Father would often kill rabbits or squirrels along the road, and we had fresh meat to cook over the campfire. We never traveled on Sunday as Father said the horses needed a day's rest. Sometimes the traveling was miserable; other days it was fun—at least for us children.

My parents settled on a raw 40 acres of rough timberland south of Forsythe, Mo. We lived in a rented house. There was plenty of timber, with walnut and white oak for good straight logs. When Father had the logs ready, neighbors from all around came and put up the logs for walls. They built one large room with an upstairs and a lean-to kitchen. Father split shingles out of burr-oak blocks.

Back of the house was a cedar glade, with beautiful trees and a good spring. We toted all our water, and when it was warm, Mother took the washing to the spring, carrying the tub, boiler, washboard, and clothes.

In the timber there were wild animals and game, and we found wild berries, plums, and grapes for jellies and jams. Father hunted for bee trees and cut them, claiming the good pure honey. Our little garden on the ridge never did much good even tho we worked hard in it.

One evening Father came in from farm work, tired and weary, and said, "If I could sell this place for enough to get back to Kansas, we would go." He did sell, and we started back in June.

The coming back wasn't so long and tiresome as we older children would walk behind the wagon, gathering flowers and wild blackberries. Only one incident stands out in my memory. Near Springfield, Mo., we were caught in a bad storm, and Father tied the wagon to the ground with a long rope to keep it from blowing over. We went to a nearby barn and slept in the haymow.

The Ozarks is beautiful country, with the dams, lakes, beautiful drives and resorts now. I have been back on vacations and I enjoyed it much more than when I lived there.

Mrs. Anna Atkinson
Longton, Kan. 67352

Rats Were Seed Thieves

My parents first settled in Stevens County, Kansas, where they built a dugout and then a second dugout when the first one fell in.

Despite the drouth in 1888, they tried to plant a corn crop. Dad plowed the ground, and on the third trip around Mother would follow, dropping seed into the furrow. Before Dad could come around again, the rats had eaten a lot of the corn.

One year later Dad was in Oklahoma to take a homestead in Payne County. He built a one-room log house there and later a larger house where the first Sunday School in the Cimarron Valley community was held. Dad later helped build a church called Hopewell. It was no unusual sight to see men go to church barefooted.

My parents triumphed over many hardships. In 1890 and 1891 Dad drove his team to Andauer, Kan., and found work at 50 cents a day. Mother earned a little money with eggs. She would buy a pair of stockings for one child, then a hair ribbon for another, but by the time she got around, the first one was needing something again. I remember one summer when she received only three cents a dozen for eggs.

Mrs. Beulah Wright
Montebello, Calif. 90640

Boy's Work—and Lots of It!

My wife talks of the enjoyment of life on her family's homestead in Las Animas County, Colorado. But I can remember nothing but hardship on my folks' homestead in what is now Alfalfa County, Oklahoma. I was eight years old when my father staked his claim, and I lived there until I was 16.

We were poor! People nowadays cannot imagine how poor we were. Cash was terribly scarce; the butter and egg money was pitifully small, with butter selling for six cents a pound and eggs for three cents a dozen.

We children walked one-and-a-half miles to school, but only after we had hunted up the cows, done the milking, and taken care of the hogs. In summer the corn and the garden had to be hoed continually to conserve the precious moisture. The hardest of all jobs was pumping water for the stock. The animals drank more in the hot, dry season, and it seemed the pumping was a never-ending job.

The cows grazed in every direction, the crop and garden lands being the only fenced lots. Our own legs had to carry us when we went out to find them. Sometimes three boys went in three directions—usually the wrong directions first.

I had even more trouble with cattle. Father took in cattle for me to herd with ours. I had no horse, and our big part-Newfoundland dog, Ponto, had no cow sense. However, he was good company and would guard me from rattlesnakes when I lay down to sleep while the cattle were resting.

What do I remember of my days on the homestead? Hard work, little play, poor food, bare feet most of the year, and compassion for my overworked mother.

Arthur E. Hoisington
Flippin, Ark. 72634

The Wall Came Tumbling Down

When I talk about the hard times on our claim in western Oklahoma—we moved there in 1906—folks think I read them in a book!

We hauled our drinking water three miles and it sat under the sun in a barrel for a week. It got good and hot.

We lived in a dugout about six years, then built out on a hill. And none too soon! On our last morning in the dugout the side fell in and buried our breakfast.

Mrs. Rosa Plowman
Altamont, Kan. 67330

Quick Surgery

In pioneer days, my grandmother lived in a sparsely settled community in Illinois. She had a small flock of chickens of which she was very proud, but she had only one rooster and did not know where she could get another.

She went out one spring morning to plant sweet corn—and garden seed was very scarce. When she had worked to the end of the row, she looked back to see the rooster had picked up and swallowed every kernel of corn she had dropped.

This resourceful young woman grabbed the rooster and rushed to the house where she collected a sharp knife and needle and thread. Without a moment's hesitation, she slit open his crop and rescued her precious seed corn. Then she sewed his crop with needle and thread. Thus she saved her corn as well as her valuable rooster which soon recovered and was none the worse after his unusual operation.

Estella Robare
Sparks, Neb. 89431

Paid in Produce

In the winter of 1898 my parents set out to take a homestead in Oklahoma. By the time they paid the filing fee, built a dugout, and bought a few pieces of furniture, the money was nearly gone. But they were not discouraged.

Father went to work helping the farmers put up fences and buildings or doing whatever they had to do. They were nearly as poor as we were, so often they had no money to pay for the work. But most of them were honest, and they gave a pig, a calf, a few chickens, or maybe a bushel of grain, turnips, or beans in exchange for his labor.

With three small children, Mother could not "work out." But she was one of the few women who had a sewing machine, so she sewed for many neighbors. She sewed so quickly and so beautifully that they paid her an enormous wage—15 cents an hour.

With both parents working, it was only two years until we could afford to build a little log shanty on the claim.

Mrs. C. H. Campbell
321 Lincoln
Ordway, Colo. 81063

109

Hard-time Gravy

Money was scarce and groceries were high when we were living on a homestead in 1919. We had grown up in the Midwest where we could have a big garden, but here in the Colorado mountains, the growing season was too short for many vegetables we had been used to.

One day a neighbor called, and I mentioned that I didn't know what to have for supper.

"Try hard-time gravy over fried potatoes," she suggested. I had never heard of it.

Here is how it is made: Dice bacon in a heavy skillet. (We used pieces off the ends of a slab; it came cheaper.) Empty half a can of tomatoes into the bacon and fryings, and simmer until it thickens. Add two or three tablespoons of flour and water, and cook like gravy. Season with salt and pepper. I add two teaspoons of sugar.

Our boys never tired of it. They said there was nothing better after walking three miles from school than to find a supper of fried or baked potatoes and plenty of hard-time gravy.

Mrs. M. E. Bouton
Oak Creek, Colo. 80467

Early Settlers Were Self-sufficient

The stories my father told of the privation and making-do which he knew in his youth over 100 years ago make me feel ashamed when I am tempted to complain of my lot in life. I'm not wealthy, but I would be considered so by the standards of those early days.

His mother, he would tell us, spun the yarn, wove the cloth, and made all her family's clothing by hand, and with the help of his sisters, she knitted, from homespun yarn, all the socks and stockings.

Each member of the family got one pair of shoes a year, and they were the crudest things imaginable, cut from rough leather and unlined.

The family usually lived in a one-room log house. They raised almost all of their food except the wild game which they hunted. Food was cooked in the fireplace the year round. They made their own soap from fat scraps and lye, and they molded candles from beef or mutton tallow.

The only refrigerator they knew was the old springhouse where they kept milk and butter and other perishables.

And in my father's early life, safety pins were unknown, even for the baby's diapers.

I could go on, but the things I have mentioned are sufficient to make us count our blessings today.

Mrs. Alice M. Disher
Portageville, Mo. 63873

Pioneering in the '30s

We lived in western Oklahoma during the Depression, and life then was much like that in pioneer days. My father raised sorghum and dried it on large mats set up on the creek out of the wind. The women helped with the grinding, cooked for the hands, and filled the buckets with molasses to be stored on our cellar shelves.

We raised black-eyed peas and little navy beans, and picked them like cotton, filling our cotton sacks. It was my job, with my brothers, to stomp the sacks, which would shell the beans and peas, and then help the wind blow the pod parts away. To this day I don't like either peas or beans.

Our home was sold from under us and we really pioneered that winter. We lived in a covered wagon and a tent which was pitched beside the wagon and had a big wood stove in the middle for heat. My father sold black-jack wood and we ate squirrels and rabbits for meat. On Thanksgiving day we had possum and noodles!

Mrs. Laverne Furnish
Star Route
Guymon, Okla. 73942

111

CHAPTER 9: Those Wonderful Women!

Grandma Loved Chickens

In her New York state home, Grandmother loved poultry, so when she came West she was anxious to have chickens. She rode 36 miles in a lumber wagon to get a setting of hen eggs, which she slipped under a wild duck setting near her home. The newly hatched chicks were brought to the house and kept inside for several weeks before they were put outside the door to pick. She saved every crumb from her table for her little brood. And once when a bobcat tried to steal a fryer, Grandmother saved her chicken by belaboring the cat with her broom.

Minnie J. Sellens
Willow Springs, Mo. 65793

Thief in the Ranks

In 1864 my grandmother lived on a cotton farm in south Missouri. The men in her family were away, fighting in the War Between the States which was nearing its close. Renegades, bushwackers, and stray soldiers came by each day, alone or in groups, northerners and southerners.

Once a captain stopped with 12 footsore, ragged soldiers, asking for provisions. The men spread thru the house to search for food and soon found there was none.

As was usual after such marauding, Grandmother looked over the house at once; she found her comb, an item hard to come by then, was missing. She called the captain and told him, and he assembled his 12 men and requested the man who had taken the comb to step forward and hand it over. The comb was recovered.

Grandma, a religious person, scolded. "What a sinful thing to do! Why would you have a thief in your ranks?"

The captain turned calmly to Grandmother and said, "Lady, even Christ did not pick 12 honest men."

Gus Lasswell
11339 Hickman Mills Drive
Kansas City, Mo. 64134

A Lady Wore Shoes

My great-grandmother and great-grandfather came to Missouri from Tennessee in a covered wagon.

Great-grandmother pulled off her shoes and walked barefoot behind the wagon, to ease the wagon weight for the oxen and to save her shoes. She would put on the shoes to walk over the roughest spots.

But Great-grandmother was a lady, and when her shoes wore out she would not enter a town barefoot. Her husband noticed this, and one night when they had camped near a village, he stole into town and with the aid of the local shoemaker, selected a pair of almost worn-out shoes. The next day Great-grandmother went to town in style, wearing her new worn-out shoes. She walked into the shoe shop and proudly bought herself a new pair.

Doris Virginia Reed
Route 1, Box 122
Washburn, Mo. 65772

Riding the Plains in a Rocking Chair

Comora Martin stayed in Missouri when her husband came to Barber County, Kansas, in early 1884 to build a shanty on his claim. In May of that year, she and her six-month-old daughter set out to join him. They traveled by train to the end of the Santa Fe line at Harper, Kansas.

The shanty had not been completed and William Martin needed more lumber. Planning to haul both lumber and family in a single trip, he had come to Harper driving his team of horses hitched to the running gear of his wagon.

When they set out for the return trip, Comora, holding the baby in her lap, was seated in a rocking chair which had been securely suspended on ropes between lengths of lumber stacked on the stripped-down wagon. The ropes served as springs. Another comfort was an umbrella tied to the rocking chair to protect mother and baby from the Kansas sun. In this unusual conveyance the Martins traveled 45 miles in a wearisome all-day trip to William's father's house where they would stay until their own house was completed.

Mrs. L. M. Stone
617 North Bluff
Anthony, Kan. 67003

When 40 Miles Seemed Like 400

My mother was alone on the homestead in Nebraska, my father having gone to Kearney for supplies, when my oldest sister, Alta, squatted down close to a rattlesnake and it bit her. Mother slashed the bitten place and sucked out blood.

Then she took her three children with her on horseback and rode to the nearest neighbor where she left two of the children. With Alta she started to Kearney and the doctor. She would ride until her horse was tired, then change to a fresh horse at the next homestead. She rode 40 miles to Kearney, but she used to say it seemed like 400 miles.

When she reached the doctor he told her she had saved my sister's life.

Inez Wade Coleman
West Point, Iowa 52656

Grandmother Kills a Snake

When Grandma Stedman came to live with her son in Kansas, she found life far different from that she had known in her native England and in New York State. Not wanting to admit her son's home was a soddy, she wrote to her other children, "We live in a prairie flagstone house."

But she took things in stride. One spring day a snake crawled out of the sod wall toward the fire. She just rocked forward and when the snake was under her chair, she rocked back and severed it.

Mrs. Adolph Musil
Home, Kan. 66438

Wore Their Coins

My grandmother told me this story: She and my great-grandmother crossed the plains in 1865 loaded with their money. Their petticoats were quilted in squares and every square had a $20 gold piece sewed in it. I forget how many thousands of dollars the women carried in their petticoats.

Bandits came to their camp one night and searched everything, but did not find the gold. The money was successfully "worn" from Montana to a new home on the Coonskin River, between Pittsburg and Wier City, Kansas.

Hattie Backman
Route 3
Rich Hill, Mo. 64779

Mother Was the Heroine

My father was away from our Holt County, Nebraska, home when Mother saw the large billowing cloud of smoke to the north. It could mean only one thing—prairie fire!

Perhaps the most effective way to combat grass fire is to burn a fire guard, that means burning a strip ahead of the oncoming flames. A border, such as a furrow, is required on the leeward side.

Mother acted quickly. She and my brother Eban, 11 years old,

115

harnessed the horses and hooked the team to the plow. With Eban driving the team and Mother holding the plow handles, a single furrow was started. It was to be the salvation of our buildings and the tons of hay in the stack.

When she had run the plow for 100 yards or so, she came back and instructed my brother Merle, nine years old, to set a fire at the side of the furrow, on the north side in the direction of the burning prairie. I had orders to keep my sister and the baby well back from the operation.

Mother and my brothers continued plowing and setting back-fires for about a mile, until they met a group doing the same thing. In the meantime, another group coming from the other direction, had arrived at Mother's starting point.

The barrier had burned 50 to 60 feet wide when the big fire arrived. It burned out.

My father came in with one of the fire-fighting groups. He called all together for a prayer. Then all were served coffee. Loud cheers arose from the crowd for my mother, the heroine of the day.

Carl W. Moss
2112 Harlan Street
Denver, Colo. 80214

Fresh Air Was the Miracle Drug

Grandmother had a touch of consumption as a child, so the doctor told her parents to keep her in the open air as much as possible if they expected her to live to be an adult.

So she milked cows, fed pigs, took a team to the fields, and cut wheat and oats with a cradle. When she married at 24 years, she could tie an 18-inch ribbon around her waist, and she could also shoulder a two-bushel sack of wheat and carry it up the stairs to the granary to dump it into a bin.

She taught school, walking nine miles to the schoolhouse in two hours, timing herself with a watch which she could check only at the depot once or twice a month when she went to town to trade.

After several of her five children were born, she again had a spell of consumption. The doctor advised her to wash her chest with cold water and beat it with her fists until it was red and warm. Some mornings her husband could hardly break the ice in the pan so she could wash.

Grandmother died quietly in her sleep; she was 104 years old! Except for one early year, she had lived 70 years of her life in Floyd and Mitchel counties in Iowa.

Robert Bishop
Nora Springs, Iowa 50458

Friendly Snakes?

My Grandmother Zeck, a homesteader in Marshall County, Kansas, told us that before she put her children to bed during the hot summer, she took the bedding outdoors and shook out the snakes. She did that so often, she said, that she and the snakes became friendly. They slithered away, only to return and drop thru the roof again to the cool interior of the sod house.

Mrs. Henrietta Swim
Marysville, Kan. 66508

Saved by the Rough Road

About the turn of the century, in the horse and buggy days, my mother-in-law often hitched up her team and drove to see a tenant family who lived about a half mile away.

As she entered the house, one day, she passed a mop pail and glanced at what she thought was a mop rag hung over the rim of the pail. On second look she saw it was a toddling baby who had fallen into the water.

My mother-in-law herded her two children and the tenant mother and her brood into the buggy and started a ride of several miles to town and a doctor, driving the horses over the rutty roads as fast as they could go. She later declared she never heard anyone pray as hard as the little mother did all the way to town.

When they reached the doctor, the baby vomited, and the doctor said the bumpy ride had saved his life.

Mrs. John Jacobs
Rudd, Iowa 50471

Spooky Companions for a Bride

One day after my husband and I were married, we left Oklahoma for Akron, Colo., riding behind a team of mules my husband was breaking in. The first night we camped beside a river near a dead tree. Thomas fed the mules and tied them to the wagon wheel. As soon as it got dark, they broke loose and started back the way they had come, straight across the prairie. Thomas trailed them, carrying our lantern.

I was a pretty scared girl. I had no light, and the dead tree was full of big black birds that cried "Caw! Caw! Caw!" I thought they would be in the wagon after me any minute.

Thomas didn't get back to our camp until after daybreak. He had followed those mules five miles before he ran them into a barn and left them for the night.

Mrs. Ethel McAlary Lasater
North Myrtle Route, Box 190
Myrtle Creek, Ore. 97457

Dough Boy

My mother, a homesteader in Nebraska in the early 1880s, was called to a neighbor's home to help deliver a baby. It was her first time to attend the birth of a child solo. In her excitement she cut the navel cord a trifle short and it started to bleed badly. Mother reached into the dough pan, pinched off a chunk of dough, stuck it on the baby's navel, and applied a tightbinder.

The baby lived and was always called "Dough Belly George."

Inez Wade Coleman
West Point, Iowa 52656

Rifle at the Ready

During the proving-up period on their claim, my parents were so short of money that my father went to the coal mines to work, leaving my mother and the children at home. Before he left, he bought a rifle and told Mother to stand it by the bed every night so it would be handy should she ever need it.

One moonlight night a noise woke Mother, and she could see what appeared to be an arm and a hand at the window screen. She reached for her gun and said, "Who is it?" Our horse whinnied. He had come for a drink from the barrel near the window.

Mrs. Pearl Allen
Route 1, Box 237
Olney Springs, Colo. 81062

'Mother, We Ain't Got Much'

Here is a letter written by my grandmother to her mother. There is no date or place on the letter, but I believe the year would be 1880 and the town Minneapolis, Kan., as the family moved from near Plymouth, Ind., to central Kansas in 1879.

Grandmother evidently had little schooling, but she wrote in this letter all the heartbreak of a woman who had moved from a land of green pastures, gardens and fruit, to the dry wilderness and who was faced with hardships almost beyond her strength to endure. Some punctuation has been added and some spelling changed to make the letter easier to read:

Dear Mother, I will try to write you a few lines to let you know some of Kansas's hard times. The first things all mostly dried up. Things that Will put in Jim's garden the chickens ate up and we didn't get a taste, and what he put out in ours, the pigs are trying to eat. We won't have any garden truck at all, but it seems so hard to live on bread and butter and coffee. And when—takes his cow away, then we can go it dry, but there's nothing here.

Oh, Mother, why did you let Rob buy such a place for his

home? I tell him he is building a prison for me. Oh, what have I done that my punishment is so great?

We ain't bought anything much yet, and we can't, for things are so high. We got a stove, and Rob made a table and we have one chair, the one we had with us, and we bargained for a dozen chickens. So, Mother, you see we ain't got much.

Rob and I and Frank and the three little ones ain't had a penny spent for clothes this summer, and that ain't all, for we ain't got somebody to send us clothes all the time.

Helen has been sick for two weeks. She lost a baby. It was only seven months, and it didn't live but a little while, and she is so she can sit up now and is doing well.

Ida looks so bad and poor. She ain't felt well all summer. She will come home when Mary comes. Anna has been working for Converse. She worked there six weeks and he won' t pay her and I don't know what we will do. He ain't so nice as he was last summer when he was taking Rob round on his land . . . Will is working for John Roy.

Mother, this is the fourth time I have tried to write to you, but when I would think of you and home I could not. Mother, I have shed many tears since I have been here but nobody cares for me. I beg of Rob to try and sell for, Mother, I can't think of staying here. About the time I had my family raised, then I must be drug out here to be deprived of almost everything. Mother, I used to think that there was one sunshiny day for me, but they are all dark.

Charley is as bad as ever. He is so poor. And I am sick most of the time.

I must stop for you will get tired for my hard story. So goodbye, Mother. From Marie Stanley.

The year after this letter was written her twelfth child in 23 years was born.

That child was only 12 years old when Grandmother died at age 53.

Mrs. O. C. Frantz
Route 2
Rocky Ford, Colo. 81067

Lamp Was Her Protector

As a child I loved to hear my grandmother talk about the "olden days" when she and Grandfather homesteaded southeast of Foss, Okla.

They had just finished building their small home and had not hung the door yet. Grandmother was sitting, waiting for Grandfather to come home. He walked to Foss every day to work for a dollar a day, and walked home each evening. In the twilight she rocked the baby, with her small daughter on a stool at her feet and a lighted lamp on the table.

When the dog whined, Grandmother glanced toward the door. There stood a huge timber wolf, growling.

Grandmother shoved the little girl out of the way and tossed the baby on the bed. She grabbed the door and held it in the doorway. The wolf left. Grandmother always thought it was the lighted lamp that kept the wolf from walking in.

It wasn't long until Grandmother had Grandfather hanging that door on hinges so it could be opened—and shut.

Mrs. Ralph Roll
Route 1
Arapaho, Okla. 73620

She Learned Early About Hard Work

My mother worked hard all her life; she never had any luxuries or conveniences, never complained of hardships. I never heard her wish for anything better than what she had.

She told us how her father called his children out of bed at three o'clock in the morning to go with him across the mountains in Arkansas to work in the cotton fields. They had a long ride by horseback and they wanted to be in the fields by daybreak. Often, she said, she would go to sleep as they rode along, but other children riding the same horse would catch her and keep her from falling. She was only 10 or 12 years old at the time, but some of her brothers and sisters were younger than that.

Mother hoed corn from the time she was six years old. And after she was married at 16, she still worked in the fields. She sat up many a night until midnight spinning and weaving by candlelight for she made the clothing for her family of 11 children. And she was up before daylight the next morning to take her place in the field, leaving her little ones in the care of one of the children, and taking the others to work by her side.

She carried her washings to the creek close by, gathering dead limbs and building a fire on the rocks under the tub to heat the water. She did her washing on a washboard and dried the clothes on bushes. While they dried, she went home to cook the dinner, maybe gathering a mess of greens along the way.

She worked hard until she was 80 and passed away when she was 90.

H. M. Groves
416 South 16
Bethany, Mo. 64424

Flour Sacks and Shirttails for the Little Ones

When I came to this community in Kansas as a bride in 1913, 1 soon had friends among the women who were pioneer wives and mothers. I liked to listen to their stories.

As young wives, they often prepared a bundle of baby clothes to be given to an expectant mother. Money was scarce, so little garments were made from men's faded blue shirttails or the best parts of wornout dresses. Diapers were mostly flour sacks. Each woman added what she could, washing and mending any baby clothes she had, and passed the layette on to her neighbor. The babies looked as sweet and dear in the hand-me-downs as they would have looked in fine linen and lace.

One friend told me of the birth of her son in their dugout home. A blizzard came up and left a blanket of snow on her bed, but she and the babe were snug and warm under the covers.

Another told how frightened she and her children were in their sod shanty when a herd of buffaloes came rushing across the prairie on their way to the river. At the soddy the herd split and passed on each side of the house without harming it.

She also told me how her family hungered for garden stuff after the grasshoppers ate everything. All was gone; where the onions had been there were only holes in the ground. Her family wanted trees so they planted precious seedlings and watered them by putting water in a washtub, tying a rope to the handle and pulling it to the little plants.

When Indians were in the country, the settlers would go to Fort Kanopolis and stay until they left. One friend told how the Indians came to their home wanting feed for horses and how her anxious father held her, a little goldenhaired girl, while the chief fingered her curls. "Little princess," he said, and left the family unharmed.

Mrs. Irma M. Folck
Sandstone Rest Home
Little River, Kan. 67457

'I Did a Lot of Growing Up'

As a 20-year-old bride, I went to live on a homestead south of Ft. Morgan, Colo. My husband had filed claim to a 320-acre tract in 1909, a year before we were married. He built a small 10 by 12-foot house there, and after I arrived, he added a 12 by 14-foot half-dugout.

For two years after our baby daughter was born, she and I stayed on the homestead while Bob worked on a ranch. It was a large ranch with about 1,000 head of cattle and 500 horses. My husband worked for $30 a month, and it was like getting blood from the proverbial turnip to collect his wages from that tough, bewhiskered old rancher. When Bob would ask for his monthly wages, Old Mike would exclaim, "Hell, Laddie, why didn't you tell me you was goin' to need money so I could've made provisions for it!" The old duffer was wealthy, but hated to turn loose of a dime.

In his barn Old Mike kept three saddle horses ready for riding.

There was Trix, a beautiful white mare with a gait as smooth as a rocking chair; Brownie, a horse that could shake your teeth even when he was walking at a slow pace; and Mile-Hi, a long-legged sorrel that could outdistance anything on the ranch. To be caught out after dark on the fenceless prairie with Mile-Hi or Brownie could prove disastrous, for they would travel in circles all night. But Trix would bring her rider home on the darkest and stormiest nights. Her homing instinct was amazing.

Bob's brother worked on another ranch during roundup time. The owner's wife did the roping; the men did the branding. Few men could match her when it came to swinging a lariat. She was a large woman, but attractive and feminine in spite of her size, and it was a marvel to watch her working the calves, riding a large brown horse she had trained herself.

The prairies were beautiful in spring and early summer, with the green buffalo grass and the cacti with their pink and white and yellow hollyhock-like blossoms. The cactus needles were wickedly sharp and stiff as nails. You were no longer a tenderfoot when you had learned to walk across the prairie without getting your shoes full of needles.

Everyone was advised to carry a snake stick when walking on the prairie as diamondback rattlers were numerous. One day when I had forgotten my snake stick I met up with a rattler. I took off my shoe and killed it.

Prairie-dog towns were numerous. The little animals built high mounds of dirt which were packed as hard as concrete. We always knew when a blizzard was coming as the prairie dogs would cover their homes.

The schoolhouse was located on our homestead, a half mile from the house. We had Sunday School on Sunday mornings and occasionally church in the afternoons. Dances were held in homes, and Bob played the violin for round and square dancing. For those who did not dance, there were party games.

We considered ourselves fortunate to have a well that supplied us with clear, sweet water. Many homesteaders had only alkali water or none at all. Alkali water was not fit for human consumption; one drink of it was equal to a king-size dose of Epsom salts.

Prairie hay was cut and stacked for winter feed with a strong fence around it to keep out the range stock. Sometimes corn would be cut and shocked, but we could never depend on the dry land to produce a real crop.

I was not sorry to leave that treeless prairie land. I learned there to cope with duststorms, rattlesnakes, and the loneliness which comes in not seeing another human soul for days. I did a lot of growing up in those years, for a Colorado homestead was a good place to learn to stand on your own two feet.

Mrs. Robert Harvey
508 South Elm Street
Lenox, Iowa 50851

CHAPTER 10: Life's Main Events

Born at Home

Over 100 years ago, so the story goes, my great-grandparents traveled from the East to homestead land in Iowa. A new child, the sixth, was expected soon, and when the family came to the last town before their destination, it was thought wise for Great-grandmother to remain there until after the birth. She agreed.

But after the rest of the family had gone, this pioneer woman decided it would be more fitting for the child to be born on their own land. She literally hitched a ride with a family traveling westward and completed the long trip lying on the floor of a lumber wagon.

And so my grandmother was born at home, in the chilly dawn of an August rainstorm, in a leaky covered wagon. She was the first white child born in Bremer County, Iowa.

Mrs. George Wessendorf
Storm Lake, Iowa 50588

Baby-catching

The one thing that stands out when I recall our years on the homestead in Logan County, Colorado, is my mother's "career." She often assisted at the delivery of a child.

As I recall, all babies arrived in the dark of night. Late, often quite late, a man, either the expectant father or the hired hand, would drive up and say, "Could you hurry, ma'am, it's pretty close..."

Mother would snatch up a sack of white cloths she kept handy, and say, "You girls be good and help your Pappy." Then she was on her way.

If the call came late at night, after we were asleep, our father would tell us at breakfast, "You girls do these dishes and be quiet if Mama is sleeping. She was up all night. Baby-catching again!" I think he resented it a bit, but Mother was always so proud of being able to help. If the baby was a girl, it likely was named Margaret in her honor. I wonder how many Margarets were born in that county in 1908 and 1909.

Babies born in modern hospitals may have a better chance to live, but none ever receive a more joyous welcome than those born in pioneer homes.

Mrs. M. Christoffersen
Powell, Wyo. 82435

Blizzard Baby

Three weeks after my parents arrived in Kansas in February of 1880, a terrible blizzard struck. My father had erected a building that he intended to be a barn, but the family was living in it, hoping to get a house built soon. But the blizzard came on suddenly, and they had to remain in the barn—my father, my mother (an invalid, seven months pregnant), and the children.

The night of February 12, 1880, was bitterly cold when Mother told Father he had better find a doctor as she knew something was going to take place. He saddled his big black stallion which was tied to the wagon beside the shack, the only windbreak the horses had, and rode three miles to Cedar Vale for the doctor. When he arrived at the doctor's house, his horse was covered with frozen snow and appeared to be a white horse.

In less than three hours after my father returned to the barn with the doctor, a little premature girl was born. The shock and cold were too much for Mother, and she lapsed into unconsciousness. The snow drifted into the building and turned to ice; the covers on her bed were frozen to the wall. My father, a newcomer to the Kansas prairie, had an invalid wife who was unconscious, a premature baby girl, and four other children to care for in a barn.

Three days later my mother recovered consciousness and found her daughter still alive. She began rubbing the child with oil and feeding it, and somehow both mother and baby managed to survive.

I was that blizzard baby.

Flora Moore
Glencoe, Okla. 73044

Her Crib Was a Tub

When my Aunt Emma was born in Iowa in 1862, she weighed 2 1/2 pounds. Without hospitals or doctors to help, her mother created a warm crib for the little baby. In a wooden tub, which she placed on a table out of reach of the children, she laid a quilt. She filled brown crockery jars with hot water and put them in the tub with a second quilt between the jars and the baby.

The child thrived, altho my daddy described her as "no bigger than a bar of soap after a week's washing."

Her mother, my grandmother, was a "yarb" or herb doctor and was often called away from home, especially on cases of childbirth. It was Aunt Emma who kept things going at home. She was a wonderful person, very precious, and she lived to be 86 years old.

Lula Husband Bright
Route 1, Box 8
North Platte, Neb. 69101

Grandma Sees a Prairie Parade

Great-grandpa was determined to be the first settler in this section of central Kansas in order to have the pick of the land and he was. He got the only farm with a good running spring and the best land to boot.

But life was mighty lonely for the children. The only thing that varied the monotony of the wearisome sameness of daily life was an occasional herd of long-horned cattle with their colorful, but dirty, cowboys making the drive up to Abilene.

To Grandma, oldest of five children and accustomed to the social life they had enjoyed back in Iowa, the hardships and loneliness were especially distressing. She was 12, an age when a girl's friends mean so much to her, and all of hers were "back East."

The approach of the Fourth of July made her even more downcast. All she could think about were the gay picnic, pretty dresses, the parade, and all the fun the girls back in Iowa would be enjoying while she was working like a slave. The night before the Fourth she had cried herself to sleep. The next morning her mother sent her to the spring to get a bucket of water. She was so depressed she didn't even notice what was approaching up the trail from the south until the neighing of a horse caught her attention.

Up the trail, their bright blue uniforms resplendent in the early morning sunshine, came a company of United States Cavalry. To that little beauty-starved girl it was the most wonderful sight in the world. No parade she ever saw in all her 70 some years ever equaled that long line of handsome glorious cavalry!

Her glory was complete when the head officer stopped, wished her a pleasant "Good morning," and a "Happy Fourth of July" and asked for a drink of cool fresh water from the spring. One after another, the men stopped for drinks and filled their canteens with the water. Grandma watched transfixed until the last of the long line disappeared over a swell to the north. From that day on Grandma loved the Kansas prairies.

Lydia Mayfield
Route 2
Halstead, Kan. 77056

A Time of Togetherness

In 1910 when we moved to our homestead in northeastern Colorado, there were no churches for many miles around. My parents welcomed any Sunday School worker or minister who visited in our community. They entertained him in our home so that he might hold church services in a nearby schoolhouse.

On one occasion an evangelist held a series of meetings that were well attended. Several young people made a profession of faith at those meetings.

The desire of the new converts for the rites of baptism created a need for a place to hold the baptismal service. My father had a large concrete water tank which he used to hold a reserve supply of water for the stock tank in the corral. He offered this tank for the ceremony. There was no other suitable body of water.

The sacrament took place on a pleasant Sunday afternoon. People came from miles around. Those who were participating came with their families; others came who were anxious to witness the ceremony for many had never had such an opportunity before. It was a time of togetherness.

The tank with the water partially warmed by the sun became a dedicated font for this occasion. How well I recall the minister, standing in the water, and the group of young people, which included my sister and myself, going up the improvised steps and down into the water to be immersed.

Most of the group have passed on, but for those of us who remain the event has special significance because it was an early step in our spiritual journey thru life.

Ruby Bigelow
Route 3, Box 3600
Grandview, Wash. 98930

Chivaree Is a Surprise

I remember that George and Grace Taft were married in the judge's chambers in Lamar, Colo. There were no church weddings then for there was no church; there were no honeymoons for there was no money.

About two weeks after the wedding, men of the neighborhood passed the word: A chivaree at the Taft place, after the dance on Friday night.

George and Grace would be attending the dance, so the others would stay on after the Tafts had gone home and had time to be in bed asleep.

The crowd went to the bride and groom's farm with tin cans strung on wire, old tubs to beat on, cowbells—anything that would make noise. We approached the house yelling like Indians.

The Tafts asked us in. A chivaree for a newly married couple was not unexpected so the Tafts were prepared. They treated with candy, gum and cigars, and Grace put a two-gallon pot of water on the stove to boil so she could make coffee. The women had brought cakes and all would enjoy coffee and cake as the party went on. They played cards or dominoes and visited, a big party for both adults and children that lasted until one or two in the morning.

Great fun!

Mrs. Louella Canfield Perkins
208 South 9th Street
Lamar, Colo. 81052

A Cake Six Layers High

I wonder how many remember the infare or second-day dinner that used to follow a wedding. My grandmother believed that such a dinner was the outgrowth of the Old World custom of feasting for several days after a special event. I went to many infare dinners as a small child. I loved the cake!

There was a lovely dinner at the home of the bride the day of the wedding, with the bride's family as hosts. On the second day the bridal couple and their guests went to the home of the groom where the infare dinner was served.

If the event took place in summer, long tables were laid under the trees in the yard, oak planks were arranged on wooden horses and covered with cloths. In cold weather the dinner was served indoors, the guests eating in relays according to their importance. Children, of course, were last.

The menu of the infare dinner might include turkey, chicken, guinea fowl, mutton and perhaps a roast shoat or two. There were many, many delicacies.

A stack cake was a feature of both the wedding and the infare dinners, and the families of the bride and the groom vied, each hoping to produce the taller cake. It was said that glass manufacturers conceived the idea of the tall, footed cake plate to lend an illusion of greater height to the cake. A serving was a very thin slice.

Neither the wedding nor the infare dinner was complete without a butter tree which was often the centerpiece on the table. Butter was pressed thru clean cheesecloth so that it came out in long curly strings. A circle of butter curls was laid on a plate and more curls added until a cone, resembling an evergreen tree, was created. The tree often was one or two feet tall.

My grandmother had a white dress with loops of light blue ribbon for her wedding day, and for the infare dinner she wore her second-day dress in dark red worsted with black velvet trim.

Alma Robison Higbee
Lathrop, Mo. 64465

A Dunk in the Creek Saved Him

My grandmother, whose life spanned more than a century, told me of laying out the dead in the parlor of their homes and putting pennies on the eyelids to keep them closed. It was an old English custom, she said.

She also mentioned a few people who were so dishonest as to steal the pennies off a dead man's eyes.

In a time before doctors were required to sign death certificates, some persons were buried before they were dead. Grandmother remembered a man who was saved when a young

132

team carrying his casket shied on a bridge and dumped the body into the creek. The water revived him.

In another case, a doctor attending the funeral of a young woman noticed a red mark under her wedding ring. He took immediate care of her and brought her out of a deep coma.

Many farmers built coffins for members of their family. They were called long boxes.

Neighbors came in to sit with the sick and the dying, and often they brought food for families in trouble. Funerals were large, often overflowing the church.

Robert Bishop
Nora Springs, Iowa 50458

'Sitting Up'

In the early part of the century, when a person died, the country undertaker might prepare the corpse in a shed at his residence. And when the body had been made ready for burial, it often looked as well cared for as if it had been embalmed in a city mortuary.

The body of the deceased was brought home for perhaps two nights before the funeral. Usually two or three friends would "sit up" near the coffin after the family retired.

One night my brother and mother were sitting up at a friend's house. While the undertaker was in attendance, he would wring soft cloths taken from a pan of salt water and place them on the dead woman's face, neck and hands. As he left he asked Mother if she would continue the treatment every two hours. "That way, Phoebe's face and hands will not turn so dark," he explained.

With my brother beside her, Mother carried on. This pioneer woman had never done such a task before, but she added it to a long list of unusual jobs she had learned to do since coming from Ohio to Kansas to marry before her nineteenth birthday.

Thelma Blosser Loucks
Route 1, Box 143
Canton, Kan. 67428

Death in the Hill Country

A small colony migrated from Georgia to the Ozark Mountains in extreme southern Missouri in the late 1860s where they took homesteads. They were hard-working, loving, God-fearing people. My father was one of them.

Twenty years later he filed on 80 acres farther up in the hills. The farms were small, and the neighbors were close and plentiful.

In the early hours of an August day, Father, Mother, and I were awakened by a banging on our door and a voice shouting, "Johnny, get up! Walter Stone is dead."

My father drew on his trousers, lighted a lamp, and opened the door to admit our nearest neighbor lady.

In a few words she explained how the son of the Stones had become ill in the night and how the younger children of that family had been sent to her home to ask that her husband ride for the doctor, six or eight miles away. She had accompanied the children back to the Stone home to offer help.

By this time Father had put on his shoes, found his hat, and was ready to leave with the woman for the Stones' house. They detoured by her home where she told her son to ride until he met the doctor and her husband and to tell them Walter had died. After three or four miles on the rough road, the son met his father and the doctor. When the doctor heard the story, he said, "I'm not needed there now. I might as well turn back." And he did.

Riding back to their home, the father instructed his son to stop at all the houses along the way, telling them the sad news. Much help would be needed, for the body could not be kept long in the heat of summer, and all preparations for the burial would be done by the willing hands of neighbors and friends. The news traveled fast, and soon many people were arriving at the Stone home, ready to help.

Mother and I rose at dawn and did our chores before breakfast. We picked green beans and dug new potatoes in the garden, and we gathered the first ripening peaches in the orchard, which Mother would make into a big cobbler.

When the food was cooked and set to cool, we combed and

braided our long hair and dressed in our Sunday clothes. I fetched our gentle mare from the meadow, and she was saddled.

Mother mounted the sidesaddle and carefully arranged her long skirts before I handed her the kettle of vegetables and the cobbler. I jumped up behind the saddle and took the kettle from Mother's hand.

When we arrived at the Stones' house, the place was swarming with men, women, and children. The whole community was there—or was coming. Mother joined the other women at the house.

I went to stand near my father who was dipping hot water over a wide walnut plank held on edge above a large butchering pot bubbling with hot water. When the plank was soaked and softened, two men gently bent the wood around a stake driven in the ground. It was nailed to a board which had been shaped for the bottom of the casket. The soaking was repeated on another plank which when properly shaped was nailed in place as the other side of the casket. Ends were fitted in place and a cover was fashioned. The men rested as the wet planks cooled, dried and set, after which all pieces were nailed together.

A bundle of black fabric was brought forth, and the rough outside was covered. The inside was carefully padded with cotton and lined with white cloth. The casket top was entirely covered with the black fabric. Last of all, a drapery of lace was pleated and tacked to the edge. Now the casket was carried into the house.

Earlier in the morning young Walter's grandmother had arrived and had held a mirror over his nose and mouth for several minutes. Finding no moisture on the glass, she had pronounced him dead.

Gentle hands had washed his body and dressed it in Sunday clothes, and now that the casket was completed, the body was laid in it. A flower was pinned to his lapel, and a Bible placed in his hands. We all passed thru the house to view the deceased.

Under the giant oak trees in the yard, a long table, made of boards on sawhorses, was set up, and a potluck dinner was served.

After dinner many of the men disappeared to their homes where they washed, shaved, and changed clothes, to reappear shortly, ready for the start to the cemetery.

The casket, carried by six or eight men, was brought out and placed in a wagon containing straw and drawn by a team of horses. People rode in wagons or on horseback or walked to the cemetery three miles away. Father joined other men on the wagon, holding the casket to protect it from jolts as the wagon traveled the rocky road.

At the cemetery a grave had been dug and a rough box placed in it. The casket was carried to graveside and the cover removed. A woman stood at the head of the casket waving a tree branch to keep flies away.

I don't remember much about the service except the singing. The preacher was the only person with a songbook. He would read a line and the congregation would sing it, and then he would read another line until the song was finished.

Everyone filed by for a last look, then the cover was put on and fastened with long screws. The casket was lowered with ropes, two men holding the end of each rope. Then the cover of the outer box was nailed in place and loose dirt was shoveled into the grave, the men tramping the soil down until the grave was filled. The preacher offered a final prayer.

Few people lingered after the close of the service. The sun was already dropping in the west and duties at home were calling us.

The day was never to be forgotten by that eight-year-old country girl.

Regie L. Vincent
P. O. Box 453
Sharon Springs, Kan. 67758

CHAPTER 11: Cows and Cowboys

Riding the Range on a Steer

On his homestead in Alberta, Canada, my father built a log cabin with an attic. We nine children all slept there and in the cold winter we played up there.

As soon as we had cattle on our farm, my brother trained a young steer to ride. Our cattle grazed on the open range, and in the evening one of us children would ride the steer to round up our milk cows.

Mrs. S. B. Ringles
Cloverdale, Ore. 97112

Cow-tested Foods

While we were proving up our claim, we had a battle to find enough food. Someone told Mother that anything a cow would eat would not poison us. So we watched to see what the cows ate, then we tried the plants.

Here are some of the delicious dishes we kids were crazy about.

Boiled soapweed blossoms. The flowers were carefully picked just before they opened; open blossoms were rejected because insects flew into them. The blooms were boiled until tender, then covered with cream and salt and pepper.

Creamed morning-glory. It was great fun to hunt for the wild morning-glory. From the time it came thru the ground until it was about six inches high, it was as tender as asparagus. The shoots were washed, boiled, and covered with cream sauce. Since this was an early spring plant, the dish was especially welcome.

Fried cactus. There was an abundance of round cactus plants. They were so covered with stickers that Mother had to pick them. She skinned off the spines and fried the center in butter, seasoning with salt and pepper.

Russian thistle "spinach." The wild Russian thistle was picked when it was young and tender, washed about a dozen times, boiled, then seasoned with bacon and salt and pepper. Served with vinegar, the thistles made the best "spinach."

Mrs. Virginia Tucker
Elkhart, Kan. 67950

Cattle Lost in a Blizzard

One summer when we lived in western Nebraska, we mowed and bunched hay for a large cattle company until late in the fall. The hay was for cattle that stayed out on the range all winter without shelter. That year we had one of the worst blizzards this county had ever known. The cattle were in good shape as they drifted with the storm, but when they came to a fence, the snow covered them and they froze. I don't know how many cattle died, but the cattle company lost heavily.

My husband got a bunch of men together and they skinned 400 head, leaving the carcasses in the fields.

The coyotes grew fat, and the big green flies were so numerous that we swatted and sprayed all spring.

Mrs. Carl E. Feikert
Kearney, Neb. 68847

'No Eat Cow Grease'

When I was just a baby (I'm now an 83-year-old woman) my

parents moved from Kansas to the Indian Territory (now Oklahoma) near Vinita and Blue Jacket.

Indians were our neighbors and I remember my parents telling of this incident.

One day an Indian came to the door to ask for something to eat. Food was scarce but Mother fixed him two sandwiches, one with jelly and the other with plain butter. He ate the jelly sandwich but refused the one with butter, saying, "Me no eat cow grease."

As a small child I slept with my parents. One night Mother woke and found I was gone. The first thing they thought was that the Indians had taken me. During their search they heard a slight whimper from under the bed. That is where they found me. In those days it was customary to lay lots of straw under the homemade rugs to make the floors warmer. Our floor was so soft the fall from the bed had not awakened me.

Mrs. Hazel Cline
315 McConnell
Joplin, Mo. 64801

No Meet Topic

To prove a claim a certain number of rods of fence had to be put up, so my father hired two young men to build fence on his South Dakota land. My mother provided dinner for the two workers, whom she described as "gentlemanly as could be, very nice boys." Of course, there was conversation around the table.

My mother recalled this incident:

"One noon as we were eating, some mention was made of how the cow had bawled that morning. One of the young men casually put the question, 'Is she with calf?'

"I froze! Never in my life had the menfolk in my family, or in any other that I knew of, raised such a question before the womenfolk. After a pause, I was able to say, 'I don't think so.'

"None of us could find a thing more to say for the rest of the meal.

"Later the cow took care of the matter herself. She broke away from her stake and for a day joined the 'wild' cattle that grazed on the unfenced prairie. My friend and I rode horses out to the range and brought the cow home where she seemed content to stay."

Lucile Houser
Route 17, Box 86
Tyler, Texas 75704

Cattle in the Crops

Our introduction to our new home in northwest Oklahoma was a windy one; the sand was blowing so hard we could scarcely see a hand before us. That home was a one-room dugout with a tent pitched in front of it. By fall we had a two-room sod house.

Cattle roamed around at will. The first summer they ate our crops as soon as the plants appeared above ground. One night Father heard them in the field and ran out in his night clothes to chase them away. They turned on him, and he made a fast retreat to our living quarters.

We tried getting good watchdogs, but the cattlemen did away with them as soon as we got them.

We children walked about a half mile to school thru a pasture where hundreds of cattle grazed. Were we ever scared when a bull showed his dislike for intruders!

In time we were able to get wire and posts to fence the cattle out.

Bertha Dobbs
205 1/2 North Eighth Street
Yakima, Wash. 98901

Horseplay at the Old Corral

The headquarters for a large ranch was a few miles from our homestead near the now extinct town of Los Tanos, Territory of New Mexico. Dad happened to be there one day when the cowboys brought in a wild horse. Each man had to try to ride him or take a spanking with a pair of chaps. My dad, being a nester, was excluded from the game.

One by one the cowboys mounted the horse and were thrown. Then one of them refused to take his turn in the saddle. He was seized, bent over a barrel, and the chaps were applied.

He fought, kicked, and cursed, and as soon as he was released he started swinging at the running cowboys. Unable to vent his wrath on tormentors he couldn't reach, he vaulted the corral fence, sprang to the saddle, and rode the wild horse to a standstill.

Dorothy Van Gundy
Wellston, Okla. 74881

Bacon Bullets

Livestock roamed thru the thousands of acres of woods in the southern part of the Missouri "bootheel" where I lived in the early 1900s.

One time my brothers put a young calf in a small building, believing the mother cow would stay nearby and they could milk her. At night the bawling of the calf and cow attracted other cattle, and they ganged up around the place and made a great commotion. Nobody could think of sleeping and nobody wanted to go outside and run them off.

Then somebody thought of shooting them to move them away. Rolled up bits of bacon skins were substituted for the lead shot removed from gun shells, and the cattle, peppered with these strange bullets, dispersed without injury.

Hazel Barton
Route 2, Highway 21
DeSoto, Mo. 63020

Huntin' Cows

Wide open range, wild range cattle, no horse, no dog—and our few cows were out there somewhere. In 1916, when my brother was 12 years old, and I, 10, and we lived in Moffat County,

Colorado, we had the job of finding the cows and bringing them home for milking.

One evening, after hours of fruitless walking, we went back without them, and our mama told us "to find those cows and don't come home without them."

We took a lantern, for it was quite dark, and we hunted. When we couldn't tell a cow from a cedar tree, we used a light from the lantern to start a small fire. We alternated resting and searching until about three o'clock in the morning when we gave up and struggled home.

Mama and our sister were in the yard calling, even shooting a gun to attract our attention. We had not heard a thing.

We really got told off! But when Mama gave an order, we thought she meant it like she said it.

Mary J. Feuerborn
343 29th Road, Route 1
Grand Junction, Colo. 81501

A Dog Saved Homes and Crops

In 1904 I left Iowa and went to North Dakota to take a homestead, hoping to teach school while I lived on my land. I built a shack there, and I did find a school only two miles away.

South of my place was a long, low range of hills covered with thick, thorny bushes. The hills were almost impassable except at an occasional gap, one of which was about a quarter mile from my place. On our side of the ridge, we raised wheat; on the other side were miles of good grazing land. Cattlemen brought in hundreds of cattle from the plains of Texas and turned them out to graze there. If the cattle ever found the gap and came into our valley, we homesteaders were lost.

One evening as I rode to my shed barn, I heard a low bellowing which could only be cattle. Quickly I pulled my horse from the buggy shafts, unharnessed him and strapped on a blanket. With Shep, a neighbor's good cattle dog, I rode wildly toward the gap. Standing on a little elevation there I saw hundreds of cattle approaching at a fast walk. At the head of the column was a mammoth bull with long horns. The bull saw Shep and me, threw up his head, stopped and pawed dirt clear over his back. With my wildest yell, I called Shep and set him on the bull. The dog knew his cattle and went for the bull's heels. Suddenly the bull started running, followed by the thundering herd. All I did was sit on my horse in the gap and shout encouragement to Shep. I stayed there until the last animal had passed the gap. Then with Shep I cantered home.

Had the cattle found the gap and turned into our valley, we homesteaders would have been destroyed. Our flimsy buildings and wheat crops would not have withstood one onslaught. Thanks to a wonderful dog, we were saved!

Jane Elmore
624 East 12th Avenue
Denver, Colo. 80203

'Borrowed' Beef

When the second schoolhouse in our Beckham County, Oklahoma, community was being built, neighbors got together and hauled lumber from Magnum, Okla., the closest rail point but still 50 miles away.

When the schoolhouse was finished, some young men wanted to have a big dance there. My Uncle August sometimes attended dances with these fellows, a couple of whom were reputed to have done some cattle rustling.

Because the fellows were afraid to ask my grandfather, who was on the school board, for permission to use the school, they put Uncle August up to doing it for them. If August could get the schoolhouse, they said, they would bring beef for a barbecue and they'd have a real party.

In the afternoon before the dance, the beef was made ready. In the evening the dance started and it lasted all night and into the next day.

When all began to say their farewells, one of the young men

asked August if he had enjoyed the dance. August said he had. The young man asked if he liked the beef. August declared the beef was really good.

A second fellow winked at August. "I thought you would like it," he said. "We got the steer out of your pasture."

Evan Fuchs
Route 2
Sayre, Okla. 73662

Point 'Em Up, Head 'Em Out!

When the Civil War started, many men who owned ranches joined the army. When they returned four years later they found the country overrun with a four-year increase in cattle. They branded the mavericks and started new ranches.

Within a few years the railroad was built to Abilene, Kan., and that town became a shipping point for cattle. The longhorns came north across the Red River, thru what is now the Kiowa and Comanche reservations, then into Cheyenne and Arapaho country. They crossed the treacherous South and North Canadian Rivers, went on to the Cherokee Outlet and the Salt Flat, then 25 miles farther to the Kansas border and north to Abilene.

As new rails were laid, other towns such as Wichita and Dodge City replaced Abilene as the destination of the cattle drives. About 1880 the Santa Fe laid rails to Caldwell, Kan., and soon it was a rip-roaring town. Cowboys from the trail herds got drunk, shot out the street lights, and rode into saloons ordering whiskey for themselves and their horses.

I held point on a cattle drive to Caldwell, and I'll tell you how a trail run was conducted.

A herd of 2,000 to 3,000 would string out about a quarter mile wide and about a half mile long. Two pointers at the head, five or six flankers on each side, and two or three young would-be cowboys, the drag drivers, at the rear, moved the herd. Besides the cowboys, there were the trail boss, the cook and the horse wrangler.

The wrangler herded the horses at night, bringing them into camp about sunup so the boys could rope their mounts for the day. Each rider was allotted four head besides his own horse. When the horses were turned in with the herd, the wrangler slept in the chuck wagon and helped the cook when we stopped for water and chuck.

The herd moved at a rate of 10 to 12 miles a day, grazing along the way so they would be in good shape when they arrived at the shipping pens. At times we traveled faster in order to get to good bed grounds and water by nightfall. If the cattle had no water during the day, they were hard to bed down and more likely to stampede. After the herd bedded down, if the cattle had had good water and grazing during the day, only one man worked the night shift. But on stormy nights it was everybody out! Should the cattle stampede, each man followed a bunch until they stopped. He would hold them until morning, then bring them back to camp.

The night shifts on the bed grounds were divided by the number in the crew. Each man on night guard roped his horse and staked him out to be ready for his shift.

The chuck wagon carried food and the boys' bedrolls. The chuck would be beans, flour, bacon, coffee, sugar, and if the owner were a generous guy, a few cases of fruit, peaches or apricots probably. The wagon was fitted out with bows and sheet, a 5- or 10-gallon keg of water on each side in case of emergency, and a dried beef hide stretched under the wagon to carry wood and the Dutch ovens used to bake biscuits. Some trail cooks made sourdough biscuits, but the general run used baking powder. In the rear of the chuck wagon there was a cupboard the width of the wagon and about five-and-a-half feet high, with shelves for the supplies and a drop-door cover. Cook used the door for his table.

While getting the chuck ready, a good cook on a trail drive seemed to be the boss, but when a question came up about crossing a bad stream or anything pertaining to the welfare of the herd, the trail boss made the decisions. At roundup in the spring it was the same; the boys just carried on with the cook. You would find men in both crews who were trail wise, but they had had an accident, maybe broken some bones riding a bad bronc, so they took a job cooking.

You could work a lifetime on a ranch and there would be tricks you still didn't know about handling those longhorns.

Joe Wiedeman
Caldwell, Kan. 67022

CHAPTER 12: When Folks Got Together

'He' Came Thru Nobly

It was my grandfather who homesteaded land in Lincoln County, Colorado, in the early years of this century. In 1915 my father took over the place, by that time a cattle ranch, with our dwelling in the town which had grown up on both sides of the Union Pacific railroad. There were stockyards, a section house, two frame school buildings, two general stores, a post office, and a scattering of dwellings.

Most of our fun included the whole family. A so-called literary society met in the schoolhouse at night. There would be debates for the big folks and recitations for the little ones. One of the debate topics that I recall was "Resolved: That the Sandy Side Is Better Than the 'Dobe Side of the Big Sandy River." The "river" was the sometimes dry, sometimes flooded stream, edged by cottonwoods, that bordered the town.

Box suppers and pie suppers were favorite activities. The women brought food enough for two in fancied-up boxes which were sold at auction to the gentlemen, the buyer sharing the contents with the supplier. It was not considered proper for the girl to hint which box was hers, but the beau seemed to have a pretty good idea of which box was whose. After all, he had carried it in, hadn't he?

One awful night I brought my pie in an elaborately frilled

basket. Imagine my embarrassment when the fancy handle flopped over when the auctioneer held it up. I felt disgraced, and was sure no one would bid on the poor thing. But "he" came thru nobly, and nobody laughed—openly!

One of our teachers put on operettas which included parents. I recall one in which my parents were in the cast and I played the piano. When my father came to his solo, he couldn't get on the key. He stood, trying bravely to find the note I kept sounding for what seemed like an age! Fortunately his part was supposed to be comic.

Sales, especially livestock sales, brought people together. The only other gatherings which incited greater response from the community were funerals. When a young woman we knew died of pneumonia, her funeral was attended by practically everyone in the county. Those poor little prairie cemeteries were dreariness itself.

We shared—perhaps that was the keynote of our lives. Great days! I wouldn't have missed them!

Mrs. John J. Pinney
Ottawa, Kan. 66067

R.S.V.P. Sent in Ribbons

Grandmother grew up on her father's homestead in Stanton County, Nebraska, where the family settled in 1866. When she was a young woman and was planning to marry, she followed a local custom in the manner in which she invited relations and friends to the wedding.

The custom decreed that the best man, chosen by the groom-to-be, had the honor of inviting the guests. Grandmother gave him a list of the families he was to call on, and he rode off to deliver the invitations personally.

At his first destination he knocked on the door and when it was opened, he announced, "William and Caroline will be married October 18. You are invited."

To signify that the family would attend the festivities, the lady

148

of the house brought out a bright ribbon, maybe 18 inches long, and pinned it to the messenger's coat.

At the next stop he made the same announcement and was decorated with another ribbon. And so he rode until all the guests had been invited.

When he came riding back to Grandmother's house, he was bedecked with ribbons, all colors and all lengths, all of them fluttering in the breeze. How she smiled!

The ribbons became a keepsake for the bride.

Mrs. Fred Abendroth
West Point, Neb. 68788

Debates Were a Friday Treat

We called them meetings of the literary society, those gatherings held on Friday evenings at the schoolhouse in the days when we lived on a 40-acre farm near Kossuth, Kan.

The program began with a debate, mostly for the entertainment of the adults. They would choose a subject, usually a funny one, such as Resolved: The Broom Is More Beneficial to the Housekeeper Than the Dishrag; or Resolved: The Horse Is More Useful Than the Cow.

Following the debates there would be a short program of readings, music, and singing.

The children in the school had their own Friday afternoon treat. If our conduct had been good during the week, the teacher would let us have spelling matches, or ciphering contests, or races to find cities on the maps in our geography.

Mrs. Hazel Cline
315 McConnell
Joplin, Mo. 64801

The Very Warm Welcome

I've heard my daddy tell how he enjoyed the contests and dances which were favorite forms of entertainment in Rooks

County, Kansas, in the 1880s. The story that amused us most took place at a dance held in a home where there were two charming young ladies.

A dude from another community came all togged out in fine clothes and fancy boots. My daddy and his pal had squired the girls for some time, and they didn't appreciate this new competition. So with the girls, they plotted to show the dude a too good time.

The girls brought out photograph albums and autograph albums, and they really entertained the guest. They sat on a big wooden tub full of cobs near the stove, one girl on one knee of the young man, and her sister on the other knee. As the stove needed stoking, first one young lady, then the other, would tend the fire, but the gentleman was never allowed to leave the tub and always one of the sisters would be with him.

When refreshment time came (about midnight), the poor guy could scarcely move. He ate and said his goodbys. He had been bested!

Lula Husband Bright
Route 1, Box 11
North Platt, Neb. 69101

Rain Couldn't Dampen the Fun

In our first summer in McPherson County, Nebraska, we attended a Fourth of July celebration at a store and post office which was close to us. A dance platform with seats around the edge had been built there. It was roofed with new lumber, but was not watertight.

People came in wagons and buggies, and some on horseback. They parked the wagons in parallel rows, with space between the lines. The horses were tied on the outside of the wagons.

In the middle, between the wagons, blankets and quilts were spread on the grass, and tables were set up. Tarpaulins over the tables kept the hot sun off.

The food was plentiful and good—all kinds of bread and rolls, cakes and cookies, pies, salads; and for meat, beef roasts, meat loaf, prairie chicken, grouse, and tame chicken.

The cowboys brought their beer and buried it to keep it cool.

Some ladies didn't have hairpins to do up their hair, so they made pins from wire and arrived with their hair arranged in the latest style, looking very pretty. The people were so friendly, and could they shake hands!

After dinner we had a rodeo, with bucking horses, races, "rasseling," boxing, and tugs of war. And in the middle of the afternoon, more people came and the dance started. Those who weren't dancing sat around the pavillion.

About dark the rain began, and the roof started to leak. The musicians played in a tent they had set up to keep their instruments dry. Some people put on raincoats, and couples danced holding umbrellas. The dance broke up about eleven. Many had miles to travel before they reached home.

Altho I am old, I remember the day as the most interesting Independence Day we ever celebrated, so different and amusing for us newcomers.

Mrs. Carl E. Feikert
519 West Eighteenth Street
Kearney, Neb. 68847

Watch for the Red Ear

In the fall the farmer went out to the cornfield with a corn knife and a shocking horse, which was a 10-foot pole with two legs on one end, about three feet tall. He would lean the corn fodder on each side of this horse until the amount was large enough for a shock, then he would throw a rope around it to pull tight and tie it with twine.

Later he would gather a wagonload of shocks and haul the corn into the barn. Then friends and neighbors would be invited to a husking bee. At the bee any man finding a red ear of corn was eligible to kiss his girl. The huskers would have cake or cookies, cold buttermilk and coffee, and anyone playing an instrument was invited to perform. The guests would dance and sing; the husking bee was a real party!

Robert Bishop
Nora Springs, Iowa 50458

Big Show at the 101 Ranch

The 160 acres my father leased in 1899 in the vicinity of Ponca City, Okla., were surrounded by the large pasture of the Miller brothers' 101 Ranch. We had to fence all sides of that quarter section to keep the Miller's cattle out.

I attended the Miller brothers' first rodeo in 1905. It was called a buffalo chase and buffalo meat was served. Thirty-three trains brought people to the pasture near the railroad track where the chase was given for the National Editors Association. Water was hauled in a thrashing machine waterwagon from a nearby creek and sold at five cents a tincup.

The Miller brothers became famous and their 101 Wild West Show was seen at home and abroad.

I remember when the Miller brothers lived in a dugout. A group of neighbors, seining for fish nearby, needed salt, so I and another girl were sent to the Millers to get it. They had us go to the cowlot and take it from the salt barrel.

Sometime later Jack Miller came to our house, wanting a drink. I drew a bucket of water and handed him a tincupful. He gave me my first dime. I was so proud. I bought my sister two yards of calico at three cents a yard. I don't remember how I spent the other four cents.

Mrs. Elsie McAllister
330 South Pine
Ponca City, Okla. 74601

Glorious Fourth

One glorious Fourth of July early in this century will always remain in my memory. We lived in a sawmill town where the log trains brought the big pine logs from the forest to be sawed into lumber, which was stacked to dry, planed, then loaded into boxcars for shipping. This was a company-owned town.

Early in the morning of July 4, the log engine was hooked to a string of boxcars and pulled to a place where company employees had gathered with their families.

When all were loaded in the boxcars, we started for the log camp, to us the greatest picnic spot in the world. Log roads were never level or straight; it seemed we were going upgrade, downgrade or around a curve all the time.

At the camp, in the shade of four giant trees, was a pine board platform, where men with a fiddle, banjo, mandolin, and two guitars waited for the dance to start. There was a stand with big jars of lemonade. A man labored over the crank of an ice-cream freezer, growling because the cream wouldn't freeze. There was an old-fashioned doll rack, and to me, the greatest attraction of all, a circle swing pulled by a mule.

I was one of seven children being fed and clothed by a father who graded lumber for $1.45 a day. That morning I left home with four nickels tied in the corner of my hanky. Before noon I spent one nickel to ride the swing. Later I spent another for a wad of cotton candy on a stick, and before starting home I bought a package of popcorn with a small folding fan attached with a rubber band.

I arrived home with one nickel still in my hanky and knew the pleasure of having money of my own for several weeks.

Mrs. Mary F. Brown
306 South Park
Aurora, Mo. 65605

Baptists Got the Bible

In the early '80s before any church had been built in Baileyville, Kan., the people met in the schoolhouse for worship. Methodists, Presbyterians and Baptists took turns.

One time the Baptist pastor could not come so sent a layman

to hold services. When the meeting opened there wasn't a Bible in the house but Scripture was quoted from memory and services were held.

A small boy, Loren Thompson, was so upset because the people had no Bible that he went to town the next morning and talked to the merchant and postmaster, Mr. Will Crow. They decided to take a collection for a Bible. Twenty-four men responded with gifts of from 25 to 50 cents, totaling $8. The Bible was purchased and they specified it was to be left at the schoolhouse but would become the property of the first denomination that built a church in Baileyville. The Bible became the property of the Baptist Church when it was dedicated June 23, 1884.

Mrs. Albert S. Hay, Jr.
Onaga, Kan. 66521

The Baby Swap

The Hutchinson Mill on the east side of the Big Blue River near Marysville, Kan., was replaced with a new and larger mill in 1867. And that new mill was to be the scene of one of Marshall County's most memorable nights.

Plans were made for a dance in the new three-story stone mill before the machinery arrived. Notices of the entertainment were sent far and wide. ,

Scores arrived for the dance, bringing well-filled baskets of food for the midnight refreshments. John Pecenka's music was at its swingin' best. Couples danced in reckless abandon, forgetting their babies sleeping peacefully in an adjoining room.

Three young single men observed the sleeping children, an even dozen bedded down on a pallet in the corner.

Then one of the trio, a twinkle in his eye, sprung the plan.

"How will they ever pick out the right kid?" he wondered aloud.

They worked fast, changing positions of the sleeping babies. Christopher's pieced quilt was swapped for Annie's pink blanket;

Billy's coverlet became Priscilla's wrap.

The mischief done, the three went their separate ways before the dance ended.

The mothers, tired from a night of dancing, wrapped the babies against the chill for the horse and buggy trip home. One young mother fretted as she rode along in the night. "I do believe Jamie has taken a cold. He sounds strange."

The husband was in the barn putting the horses away when his wife's cries told him something dreadful was amiss. Little James, his mother had discovered, was a girl.

The horses were hitched to the rig again. The nine miles to the mill seemed to take forever. At the mill, a state of bedlam reigned: parents were gathering to exchange offspring; mothers cried; babies howled.

The last exchange of babies was completed as the first rays of sunrise appeared.

Angry mothers would have meted out punishment for the perpetrators of the prank, but the culprits were nowhere to be found. Not a single baby seemed worse for the experience, and the humor of the situation soon began to surface.

Owen Wister borrowed this incident for a chapter in his novel, "The Virginian."

Vera M. Brooks
900 North Street
Marysville, Kan. 66508

A Song Long Remembered

A medicine show came to our town often in a wagon with gaudy painted sides and a back that let down to form a stage. The medicine man always had entertainers who sang, danced and played musical instruments, but all he did was hawk his wares. He always put on a good spiel; his medicine, he suggested, would make one feel young again, as well as cure almost any ailment the men and women of his audience might be suffering from.

The flickering torches lit up the scenery in the black night and made everything unreal and spectacular, coloring the wagon and the entertainers with an eerie glow.

I remember going to one show night after night to hear the girl entertainer sing. She sang a song that went with the times, for this was after World War I, and it began like this:

> "Sweet Marie, wait for me,
> in a side street in old Paree,
> In the heart of Montmartre,
> don't forget about me, cherie."

Following the chorus, she recited a verse and then sang another chorus.

I was 12 or 13 years old then and I still remember the words and the tune. I have often wondered where the song originated and who wrote it. I've never heard it since that time.

Newlon I. Griffis
Rural Route 7, Box 39
Joplin, Mo. 64801

A Most Enjoyable Fair

A neighbor came by our farm telling us, newcomers to a western Colorado homestead, about the county fair. We fixed a picnic dinner and went.

All the families spread their dinners together. People came up and introduced themselves and shook hands. No strangers—it was wonderful. There were exhibits of canned goods and fancywork.

In the afternoon we stood around some hastily built pens and watched one of the finest rodeos I ever saw. Cowboys had gone to the mountains and herded into the pens some wild horses and steers from the range. They would rope an animal and a cowboy would try to ride him. If he succeeded, someone would pass the hat and the spectators would contribute their small change. He might possibly get $1.50 or $2. If he was bucked off, he gained nothing but experience .

The celebration broke up about five o'clock so we could all get home by dark. Now in my eightieth year I think of that day, and I'm sure it was one of the most enjoyable fairs I ever attended.

Mrs. Elizabeth Fisher
Great Bend, Kan. 67530

At Grandfather's Farm

Born in Europe, Grandpa Henry Boese came to America with other Mennonites. He and his wife homesteaded between Freeman and Marion, South Dakota.

They lived in an unusual house—a house joined to a barn. The dividing wall was thick, and the barn was kept very clean. Two oxen, big, strong and slow, lived in the barn, and later cows were kept there.

How happy we were when we could go to Grandpa's house! At Thanksgiving and Christmas, when the days were cold, Mother would heat bricks in the oven and wrap them in gunny sacks to keep our feet warm during the eight-mile trip by buggy. Our cheeks would be rosy and our hands cold before we reached our destination.

At the house the women greeted each other with hugs and tender words. Grandpa had pink peppermints for each child and later we tasted his newly processed honey.

We ate on benches or on a green wooden trunk. The knives and forks had wooden handles. How delicious were the homemade bread and the ground cherry or blackberry pie! Grandpa had an orchard of mulberries, apples, currants, chokeberries and plums.

We children tested our skill in drawing water from the well in the oaken bucket. We jerked the rope to tip the pail at the bottom, and then we pulled the rope which was around a pully at the top. We competed to see who could raise the most water in the bucket. How the boys bragged of their achievements!

We made our own entertainment!

Esther Dirks Herman
Riverton, Neb. 68972

157

Home for Christmas

In the early 1900s my family, with its two small boys, lived on a homestead farm in North Dakota. Spending our first vacation in Iowa with our parents in the old farm home at Christmastime was a great joy to us. We arrived the day before Christmas, so we could be present for the program at our country church.

We rode to the church in a bobsled with high sideboards and spring seats along the sides. In the bottom was a carpet of bright straw. The team had red tassels on their bridles and a string of sleigh bells on the harness.

After walking down the aisle of the church, seeing the bright lamps in their brackets, we found a seat facing the tree. It was a big tree decorated with waves of tinsel, colored paper ropes, and ornaments. Gifts were piled at the base. After the program and music, the gifts were passed, and then the benediction closed the program.

My four-year-old son, happy with the evening, turned a somersault in the pew beside me, causing a few people to smile as he exclaimed, "Well, the show is over."

Mrs. Grace Thompson
Oelwein, Iowa 50662

Come One, Come All!

As I am an old-timer, I want to tell about old-time play parties. They were enjoyed by young and old and were our main source of entertainment.

Usually young men or women in the neighborhood, looking for diversion and entertainment, would hit on the idea of a party. They would ride a horse or walk to a friend's house and ask, "How about a party tomorrow night?" Usually the friend would be agreeable, so off they would go to other houses until every family around had been invited. The parties were neighborhood affairs.

Sometimes at a party one of the guests would volunteer to be the host for the next party and he would issue his invitation to the group. If a new family moved into the community, they would be invited, too.

Most homes were small and more often than not a bed had to be taken down or a table moved out to make room for the activities. The games we played were not much different from square dancing except that we danced to singing instead of fiddle music. We sang as we danced. None of us minded the rough floors made of native lumber. In the summertime we often played in the yard.

No one thought of serving refreshments—well, maybe a pan of apples would be passed around or at Christmas popcorn balls would be offered.

Most parents played the games with their children while others told stories or sang songs to the little folks. I had my father as a partner many times when Mother didn't care to play.

In most of the games the words of the song told us what to do and after a few tries the routines were easy and fun. Here is an example of the calls in a game we knew as Tidy-ho.

"Pass one window, tidy-ho, pass two windows, tidy-ho,
Pass three windows, tidy-ho, pass four windows, tidy-ho,
Skip to the center and bow to your beau
And we'll all go jingle, tidy-ho."

The verse was repeated for each couple in the game.

Other games I recall were Pig in the Parlor; Pretty Little Girl in Georgia; Skip to My Lou, My Darling; Old Dan Tucker; Buffalo Gal, Are You Coming Out Tonight; Evelina Roll Around; Farmer in the Dell.

The automobile and new forms of inexpensive entertainment spelled the end of play parties, but many of the songs have not been forgotten.

Anna Atkinson
Longton, Kan. 67352

CHAPTER 13: The Children Remember

Agent Called Up a Special Train

Wilson Gossett Black, my father, and Dan Dixon rented a railroad car to move from Ohio to Kansas. The horses, one team for each family, were put in one end of the car, and the household goods in the other end. The families came by train.

We had to drive 18 miles to the depot, and after we had traveled about 10 miles it began to rain. We missed the train by 10 minutes, and since we had no extra money we stayed in the depot for 12 hours until another train came. We were wet, and all our clothing was packed in the wagon. The depot agent kept a good fire going, and finally our clothes dried.

As near as I, then a child of six, can remember, the trip took two days and two nights. We arrived in Newton, Kan., December 16, 1876, about 10 p. m.

There was no train to Wichita until the next day, but the depot agent sent a messenger to round up an engineer, fireman, conductor and brakeman; a single car was hooked to an engine, and a special train was created to carry us to Sedgwick. We arrived about midnight.

The trainmen left the train on the track and went to a hotel for the night. In the morning they took the train on to Wichita, the end of the line where there was a turntable, and headed back to Newton.

The two families moved into a shack west of Valley Center and lived there—the 14 of them—for two weeks until a neighbor who had 11 children, insisted that the Black family, with four children, move into two rooms of their house.

John Black
Bentley, Kan. 67106

'Washing Down' Produced Water

All my parents' belongings traveled by rail in an emigrant car when the family moved to a homestead in the sandhills near Alliance, Neb., in March of 1899. When they arrived, Father and one son with the freight, Mother and a younger son by passenger train, they had eight dollars and some change to start a new life.

The lumber used in partitioning the emigrant car was reclaimed for a shed which was shelter for the family that first summer on the homestead. A rug covered the open front of the shed; and the roof, without shingles, leaked when it rained. In November they were able to move into a new sod house, altho the floors were not completed. When the house was finished, it had five good-sized rooms.

For grocery money they sold cream every day, driving a team of horses to deliver the day's milk at the creamery where it would be separated. The skimmed milk was brought home and fed to calves and pigs. Later, when the separator came into common use, they bought one and saved that daily trip to town.

When tracks for the C B & Q Railroad, commonly known as the Burlington Northern, were being laid from Alliance to Sidney, Father sold watermelons and fresh vegetables to the construction workers who camped near their work. Many years later we lost our hay in a fire set off by a spark from a train on that track. Our buildings were saved only by a stroke of luck as a high wind fanned the flames.

In the sandhills water wells were shallow, and water was obtained by a method called "washing down." One man would lower a sand-bucket at the end of a rope inside a pipe, and another man would force the pipe into the well as the sand and water were lifted out in the bucket. After reaching a good flow of water, they would install a hand pump, and later, if they could afford it, a windmill.

My mother taught school before she married, and when I was three years old she returned to teaching and continued 11 years. My father, whose health was poor after he came West, died in 1910 when I was seven.

Mother taught as many as 35 pupils, from six to 16 years old, for $25 a month. The schoolhouse, a sod one, was three-and-a-half miles from our home. Some pupils came as far as three miles to school, walking or riding horseback, sometimes two or three on one horse.

I recall a blizzard that struck when I was 10 or 11 years old. Snow started in the morning and only Mother and I and one other pupil went to school that day. When the weather grew worse, Mother dismissed early. The other pupil, a 12-year-old girl, walked a mile-and-a-half with the storm at her back and arrived home safely. Mother was driving an old horse hitched to a two-wheeled cart and our direction was westward into a northwest wind and the cutting snow. Mother guided Prince the way she thought we should go, but when she gave a little slack to the lines he would turn into the storm. Mother soon lost all sense of direction and realized she was lost. She let Prince have his way, and only when he stopped at a gate she recognized as one we should go thru only a mile from our house, did she realize Prince was taking us safely to our house.

I experienced several runaways. At one time Mother and I rode to school behind a big black Hambletonian mare. One evening Belle became frightened when she saw a spotted colt tied to the fence near the house. Altho the colt was wild and fitful, Mother thought she could lead our horse past him. Belle jerked loose, changed directions, crossed the alfalfa field, and ran thru a fence. I was thrown to the ground and the lines caught on my foot. I was dragged a ways.

The year 1978 finds me still living on the sandhill homestead my father chose. I wasn't there to share the early hardships, but there were plenty to be endured after I was old enough to remember. Mother once told me, while we sat under an umbrella to gain protection from rain coming thru a leaky roof in a sod house, "Bernice, you have pioneered, if ever a child has."

H. Bernice Shanklin
Alliance, Neb. 69301

A Sniff of Lye

I spent most of my childhood days at my grandfather's house on Rock Creek in Jefferson County, Nebraska, where he settled in 1869.

I recall our saving wood ashes to make soap with the dripping lye. One night the cow which was tied with a rope to a stake got loose and took a taste from the big iron kettle where the lye was held. She sniffed and snorted, and developed a sore nose.

When I was 10 years old, I had a wild grapevine swing which would carry me across a creek.

We went to town in the winter when the snow was deep on a bobsled pulled by a team of horses.

Grandfather raised 10 acres of wheat each year. He cut it with a cradle and stacked it until it went thru a sweat. Then he thrashed it with a horsepowered machine. At the grist mill where he took it to be made into flour, he would test it on the point of his penknife to see its quality. We made good bread with hop yeast.

Mrs. Ida Emery
Endicott, Neb. 68350

Campout in the Wagon Yard

My parents purchased a relinquishment in Oklahoma from a man who had homesteaded it and didn't want to stay on the land to prove it up. We moved there in 1911.

We had a large dugout, with dirt floors and dirt walls, so deep in the ground that we children had to climb on chairs to see outdoors. Daddy used to say that when the dog barked at someone approaching our house, we ran to the door and poked our heads up like a bunch of prairie dogs looking out of a den.

Everything we purchased had to be brought from Texhoma by wagon. Daddy would fill the wagon with maize heads and leave our place early in the morning. He stayed in the wagon yard in town that night and returned home the next day.

We all helped him get started. There was bedding to roll, for he slept in the bunkhouse, and there were the skillet, coffeepot, utensils, and food to pack in the grub box, because he cooked his own supper and breakfast. The eggs were placed in grain in a tub so they wouldn't break.

He was delayed one morning after I went running down the dugout steps and heard the awful rattle of a snake and saw him coiled, ready to strike. I got back up the steps more quickly than I went down. Daddy took time to get rid of the snake before he left.

Mrs. Beryl Norris
Texhoma, Okla. 73949

Homesteading in Dry-land Country

In 1898 I lived with my aunt and uncle on a homestead near Arriba, Colo., on the prairie about 100 miles southeast of Denver.

Our first soddy was cut into the earth about five feet deep, with blocks of sod around it to raise the walls about three more feet and allow for a window in every room. The roof was made of two-by-fours supporting boards and covered with more sod blocks arranged to shed rain.

The inside walls were faced with some sort of lightweight lumber, the rooms created either by curtains strung on wire or by wooden partitions. The floor was boarded over and kept carpeted in the bedrooms and living room. The result was a cozy and livable home.

Our second sod house, built in 1902, was entirely above ground. As I remember it was finished off and floored inside just as a frame house would have been. I especially remember that the deep window seats were filled with geraniums and bleeding hearts and other flowers.

Our main cooking fuel was cow chips, the hard sun-dried droppings of the cattle herds and remaining buffalo that roamed the prairie land.

About once a month, Uncle Jeff would hitch his team to the box wagon and we would go chip-picking. Sometimes we had to drive 10 miles to reach the route the herd had taken. But when we did, it was quick work to fill the wagon bed.

My cousins and I loved the job of chip-picking. Occasionally we saw some buffalo. But there was always the excitement of topping a prairie swell to come upon a herd of antelope whose powderpuff tails instantly vanished in some arroyo or dip in the land.

Then there was the fun of coming on to a badger away from his hole and watching our dogs try to catch it. They never did! Armed with extra strong claws, the badger in seconds could dig a hole deep enough to protect his rear end, and no dog was brave enough to face those claws and his teeth.

Then there were the prairie dogs, each little rodent sitting saucily atop his hilled-up burrow, barking with all his might, but ducking into his home when we neared him.

Most prairie dogs entertained two guests: a little round-faced prairie owl and a rattlesnake. Often the owl stood on the mound alongside the prairie dog and after those two had dodged into the hole, we children would use a mirror to flash light into the burrow, and we would see the rattler coiled there. The dog, owl, and snake seemed to get along perfectly together.

Due to the scarcity of rainfall, a good garden was an impossibility. Even if the plants did come up, they were almost sure to be trampled or eaten by the cattle which were replacing buffalos on the open range. All the fruit and vegetables we ate came in cans.

It was different with meat. We depended on the multitude of jack rabbits that infested the prairie. The backs and hind legs we boiled, baked, fried, and even made mincemeat of. We also managed an occasional antelope, and when the weather was cold enough to keep meat continually frozen, my uncle butchered a young steer.

Each year my uncle rounded up the cattle and horses bearing his brand. He selected the young horses ready to be broken, and for days our place resembled a rodeo. All the young neighbor boys came in to help with the breaking. When the broncos were saddle-broken, they, with the cattle Uncle wanted to sell, were driven to the stockyards in Denver. When Uncle Jeff returned, he knew to a dime what his year's labor had earned.

When my aunt developed quinsy and was bedfast, neighbors for miles around came in to wash, iron, and cook for us until she was up again. Many times my aunt did the same for one of them. People don't seem to have time for that kind of friendliness anymore.

Garnet K. Tien
11320 Sylvan Green Lane
Riverview, Fla. 33569

Giddy Up, Ol' Tumble

One thing I remember about the Colorado homestead where I was born was the blowing sand.

Another was the yellow clay my father took out of the ground as he dug a well by hand. A tablespoon of the clay stirred into a cup of water made delicious looking "coffee" and my sisters served lots of it to me in our playhouse. I always felt this was where I got all my grit in later years.

We children enjoyed the tumbleweeds. They made wonderful horses; we tied a string at the root end and they would roll along nicely as we pulled them. Papa was not always happy with our make-believe horses, for he would lead the real horses into the barn and find our tumbleweeds in the stalls tied to the manger.

Mrs. Moody Messick
1501 Alston
Marysville, Kan. 66708

Barefoot in the Snow

My father had five dollars when he and my mother were married in 1898. They started housekeeping in a one-room log cabin. I remember living in that log house. When it rained the whitewashed plaster that chinked the logs would fall out. Sweeping it up kept Mother busy.

A few years later Dad built a small side room of planks, attached to the cabin but not opening from it. We would wade barefoot in the snow from cabin to side room where we slept.

We had a homemade sled of split logs, drawn by two horses. The runners were logs. One cold day when we were about halfway to town, two gray wolves stood beside the road, acting as if they wanted to jump on the sled. They frightened our horses.

I will never forget the turkey hen Mother had setting on eggs under the floor. Every day we would raise the floor plank to see if any eggs had hatched. One day we broke an egg and it had a tiny turkey in it. We grieved over that little dead turkey.

Mrs. Ouida Parsons
North 13th Street
Tecumseh, Okla. 74873

A Welcome Trade in New Territories

In Millersburg, Iowa, Papa was a well driller by trade, but he wanted to be a farmer. In 1901 he came to El Reno, Okla., to the registration for land drawing in the Lawton District. He held a good number, but when it was called, he was ill and could not claim the land.

But he liked Oklahoma. So in 1907 he came to the land office in Woodward and bought a relinquishment, then used his filing right to homestead near Elmwood.

That year he shipped his well-drilling equipment, horses, poultry, and household goods to Shattuck, then freighted them to his farm. Mama came in a few weeks by train with the four children.

Papa used those well drilling tools. He drilled many wells around the neighborhood. The start of our herd was one cow which Papa took in part-payment for a well completed for a neighbor. He drilled our well, with excellent water at 123 feet. In 1970 when a second well was required, it had to go to 139 feet.

Fern Pounds
Elmwood, Okla. 73935

She Cherishes Memories of Soddy Days

At the age of eight, I was living with my grandparents when they drove from Manhattan, Kan., to my grandfather's claim in Finney County, Kansas, near Lobel.

A big two-room soddy was a rich man's paradise, so cool in summer and so warm in winter. Soddies were made with 20-inch slabs, and their thickness created a wide ledge below each window. Our windows held tin cans with beautiful red geraniums.

The big wood cookstove burned chips which made a good hot fire. Grandpa and I would take our pitchforks and go out on the prairie to search for chips. Under each chip we'd find a toad or two.

School was in a soddy, a mile away from home.

I wouldn't take anything for the experiences I had living in that soddy.

Mrs. Anna Allingham Parsons
Route 1, Box 36
Milo, Mo. 64767

A Song at Twilight

Looking back into a long-ago childhood, I can see in memory Mama, Dad and us children of assorted ages sitting in the yard around a smudge fire to keep the mosquitoes away in the still summer night. Mama and Dad loved to sing the old songs together: "On the Banks of the Wabash," "Soldiers of the Legion" from McGuffey's Fifth Reader; "Mary Dow, the Match Girl," "I Wandered to the Village, Tom," and "The Dying Cowboy."

Then after a day of playing around the farm, we children would wash our bare feet in the foot tub outside and go to bed, tired and happy.

Mrs. Ann M. Blincow
E. 2339 S. Altmont Blvd.
Spokane, Wash. 99202

Praying and Plowing Saved Them

The fire came sweeping across the plains, and our house, a one-room half dugout in Oklahoma Territory, seemed to be doomed. My father plowed frantically to cut the path of the fire. He had instructed Mama and Grandma to grab their most valuable possessions and run to the windmill and stand by the water tank.

My brother brought his pocket knife and marbles. I clutched my little red chair and ran with the others.

We stood in horror as the flames mocked the ever-increasing strip of plowed ground. Grandma and Mama were praying. Suddenly I began crying, and Mama thought I was hysterical. She was trying to comfort me when I explained, "I forgot my new red ribbon."

The efforts of my father and the prayers of Mama and Grandma saved our house, but even now I can feel the terror of the family as it faced near tragedy and I remember the sobs of a five-year-old girl threatened with the loss of her most treasured possession, a new red hair ribbon.

Mrs. Bobbie Kennard
Sulphur Springs, Ark. 72768

Planting Corn Was a Good Show

Timber and rocks—that's about all it was, that Arkansas farm where we lived after I was three years old.

When we went to town, we had to stop the wagon if we wanted to hear each other speak because the wheels made so much racket on the rocks in the road.

On that farm we raised feed and broomcorn, and my daddy made brooms. We grew cane and made molasses, had a garden and put up kraut and pickles, dried apples, picked and canned wild berries, and took corn and wheat to the grist mill to be ground into meal and flour. We made very few trips to town for supplies and food.

Before we came to Arkansas, Daddy bought a pump and a hand corn planter. He put the pump in our well and people thought it was the funniest thing they had ever seen. And they would come to watch him when he put in his corn with that little planter.

The black snakes were so plentiful that our parents wouldn't let us children play in the yard by ourselves. When we went to church, Daddy always walked in front of us so he could kill the snakes in our path.

Mrs. Lena Foster
Route 2, Box 7
Galt, Mo. 64641

Calico Delivered to the Door

Remember the oldtime tin peddler? On the shelves in his little wagon, he carried sweet-smelling spices, packages of Lyons coffee at 10 cents a pound, some packages of Corn Cake smoking tobacco, and bolts of pink lawn and red calico. Once Mother sent butter and eggs to the peddler to trade for the cloth from which she made the dresses we wore to Sunday School.

The peddler usually had a stick of red-stripe candy for us children. We saved our pennies and bought little tin plates with A, B, Cs in red letters or animal pictures.

We loved the peddler.

Carrie Omeara
Caldwell, Kan. 67022

China for a Tea Party

Toys were scarce in the days when my parents and we three children lived on Daddy's claim in western Oklahoma. The make-believe dishes which a neighbor girl taught me to make were a favorite plaything when I was a little child.

Half an eggshell made a lovely bowl or cup when the round end was pasted on a small circle of cardboard. We used thick flour paste so the shell would stand up. Then paper handles were attached on the sides for cups or sugar bowls.

A coffeepot was a shell with the small end cut away for the open top, and pasted on a round of cardboard. We gave it a handle and a spout on the opposite side. A cream pitcher was made the same way.

For a particularly fancy set of tea things we created gold or blue or pink banded dishes by pasting colored paper strips on the shells.

Mrs. Fred Compton
Terlton, Okla. 74801

Retracing the Old Route Is Sad

The last wave of homesteaders came into Hamilton County, Kansas, about 1907—my parents among them. Earlier homesteaders were often cattle ranchers by then, and they resented the influx of new homesteaders to the range. But one friendly rancher near our claim let my folks get water from his place until we had our own well.

By now the homesteaders chartered railroad cars to transport their goods; usually several families went together. We latecomers did not fear hostile elements, and I do not recall any brawls, threats or pistol-slinging, but the hardships and disappointments were real.

On the first trip from the town of Kendall to our new homesite, I cannot recall seeing any homes or broken sod along the way. A prairie fire had blackened the whole countryside.

Several years ago I retraced the road we traveled that day. The sandhills were ugly with weeds, the virgin sod was almost all plowed up, and the flowers were gone from the beautiful prairies. I wept at the place of the old cemetery; it had not been spared and had been seeded with wheat.

Mrs. Louise Brumfield
Jetmore, Kan. 67854

The Joy of Autumn

As a pre-school age girl, I remember the beautiful autumn days of the early 1900s at my parents' home in central Kansas. (They had established their home on the prairie in 1880.) October is the month that stands out most vividly in my memory.

The big orchard Mother had tended so faithfully was bearing abundantly. What a thrill it was for me to go with her on a crisp October morning to pick apples—Winesaps, Ben Davis, Missouri Pippins, and some with names we did not know because the nursery had sent the trees without labels. We called them the yellow sweets, the big yellow-red striped, and the speckled sweet. I have never seen some of those varieties since our old orchard died.

Before the harvest, Mother cleaned one room and removed most of the furniture. The floor was newly painted, and old clean sheets were spread out. Each variety of apples went into its own pile. How proud my mother was, when with a smile on her face, she would take a lamp and show visitors her bountiful apple harvest.

Next came the sorting. The good apples were stored in the cellar and the others my father took to his brother-in-law who had a press, and they were made into cider. Mother made apple jelly by the gallon.

On Saturday Mother baked zwieback so we would be ready for company who might stop by on Sunday afternoon. She served coffee, zwieback, jelly, and cookies.

In the outside kitchen there was an oven and hearth made of

brick. Mother burned straw in the oven until the bricks were hot, and then with a long iron fork she placed a three-footed stool in the oven. On that went a long pan of zwieback. When the zwiebacks were done, a big pan of apples was baked. How good they smelled!

After a bath in a washtub, placed in the outside kitchen, we were all set for Sunday.

Life was simple, but we were thankful for the things we had.

Mrs. Alvin Schroeder
Box 204
Goessel, Kan. 67053

CHAPTER 14: Lessons and Learning

Grandpa Believed in Education

My grandparents came to Kansas in 1878 from Plum Hollow, Iowa, to settle in the Bow Creek country near Sugar Loaf Mound. Their sons walked nearly all the way with the cattle.

For the 10 persons in the family, Grandpa and the boys built a cabin 10 by 16 feet. The furniture was put out at night to make room for their bed rolls.

Grandpa believed in education. He sent the last money the family had, a $10 gold piece, to Cousin Jennie in Iowa, asking her to come to Kansas and teach. The letter took so long to reach her and the paper was so worn from handling that the money fell to her lap before she opened the envelope.

Jennie was a wheelchair lady, but she came to teach. A small school was put up on a hill, and a three-month term was set for small, medium, and large pupils.

It was the boys' chore to cut the wood which heated the school. They made a sort of sled with wheels and each day they hauled Cousin Jennie and the fuel to school.

My father, almost 18 at the time, was one of the pupils.

Mrs. Earl Bright
Route 1, Box 11
North Pratte, Neb. 69101

Friendly Act Repaid in Release

My grandparents were early settlers in southern Kansas after they were married in 1875. One day they noticed a small band of Indians observing their cabin. Grandmother was terribly frightened, but Grandfather said to act friendly and see what they wanted.

The Indians approached and entered the cabin. Grandmother offered them food which they ate hungrily. They examined everything in the cabin, looked over the occupants, then filed out and went on their way.

Sometime later while Grandfather was on duty as a scout, he was captured by Indians and taken to their village. There he was secured so he could not possibly escape.

While he was worrying about his possible fate, a small party of Indians rode up and stopped to look at the captive. One of them said something to his companions, then went to another group to talk more. Grandfather was sure they were planning some cruel death for him. When the Indian returned, he released Grandfather and gave him a horse, saying "White man, friend." Grandfather recognized him as one of the Indians he had fed that day in the cabin.

This true story was told by my grandparents to their children to illustrate the Bible teaching which says: Cast thy bread upon the waters: for thou shalt find it after many days. My mother told it to her children; I told it to mine.

Mrs. John H. Anderson
1703 Manning
Hannibal, Mo. 63401

Honesty Earned Two Rewards

My father, William A. Stevens, learned his first lesson in honesty as a small child when his parents were moving from La Motte, Iowa, to Polk County, Nebraska.

His father was walking beside the wagon when he found a

man's leather wallet. Handing it to his wife in the wagon, he told her to count the money.

"I am not going to open it," she said. "It belongs to someone, and sooner or later, he will come looking for it."

The next afternoon a man on horseback came riding up, asking about a wallet he had lost. After he had identified the one found on the trail, Grandfather handed it to him. The stranger gave him a dollar reward and rode away.

That same afternoon the man returned, riding pell-mell toward the wagon. "Now," said Grandmother, "he'll probably say there is something missing from the wallet."

But such was not the case. The rider handed Grandfather a five dollar bill, explaining that his honesty should be rewarded. In the pocketbook, the stranger said, were his life's savings, $2,000 in bills and notes. He had counted it, and seeing there was not a cent missing, he felt ashamed that he had given so small a reward.

My father, telling the story, said he didn't know then what the tears in his father's eyes meant, but he realized in later years that six dollars was a lot of money for people as poor as they were. In fact, after Grandfather paid his homestead filing fee of $16, he had only seven dollars left to live on that first year in Nebraska.

Mrs. Mildred Stevens Anderson
Stromsburg, Neb. 68666

Letters in the Sand

I have seen many things happen and many things come and go in my 72 years, 69 of them lived in Kansas. My folks came to Haskell County, Kansas, from Carrolton, Mo., in 1909.

The year of 1914 was the time of the big Cimarron River flood here. The railroad bridge was washed out and the water surrounded our homestead but didn't quite reach our one-room house. Cattle went floating by, some dead, some alive, and uprooted trees washed up close to the house. That was the biggest flood the old Cimarron ever had.

The town of Satanta was started in 1913, and I can remember

that my mother and we children, with a friend and her children, drove to the site in a wagon to see where the stakes were laid out. I have lived in that town for 24 years now.

My father took me and my brothers to the field with him many times, and he would stop, level off sand with his hand, and make letters of the alphabet to teach us our ABC's. By the time I and my oldest brother entered the first grade we knew the alphabet.

I can also remember one early winter when my daddy put up stacks of Russian thistles and cut sunflowers for hay. Two winters he cut and sold soapweeds for a living. I helped make pens for jack rabbit drives and took part in the drive several winters when the snow was deep.

Mrs. Alice McIver
Box 601
Satanta, Kan. 67870

Fly Taught Lesson

Nearly a century ago, when a youth of 16, my dad left a comfortable home in Iowa for a squatter claim in the valley of the Loup River. He wanted change, and he got it.

He staked out his claim, broke virgin soil, and built a soddy, which had few comforts common in homes today. He did have running water, but it was rods away as it flowed down the river.

The wilderness was depressing with a wildness that nourished extreme loneliness. Dad told me this story, one which shed the light of truth on the simple events which often shape our lives:

"It was a gloomy day. Came noon and I made a meal of cornbread, beans, molasses, and coffee. A fly buzzed over the table and landed near the molasses.

"I became fascinated by the fly. The crush of my lonely mood and some compassion for any form of life caused me to look on it as a friend. I brushed the fly from the food. It took off, buzzed around my head a few times, and made another landing near the sweet stuff.

"The fly must have thought of my table as its own squatter claim; it was not going to give up to any claim-jumper such as I. He returned again and again.

"When I left that sod hut, I had been taught a lesson of courage and persistence. During the years of slavish labor on that claim, I often thought to turn tail and run, but that fly had taught its lesson well, and I plowed on."

Norman E. Graham
805 Ella Street
Beatrice, Neb. 68310

McGuffey's Reader Was Her Teacher

As a child on the quarter section farm we were homesteading in the sand hills south of North Platte, Neb., my job was to herd the chickens to keep the coyotes from eating them. A few years later I stepped up to herding sheep to keep the wolves and coyotes from eating them.

My grandparents sent us some used schoolbooks and I studied them as I herded. At night my parents heard me recite my lessons. I was soon able to read anything, so when I tell people I had no formal education, they do not believe me. But the McGuffey and Wilson readers that I studied had things in them that modern college students never learn.

When our horses died, we broke a pair of steers to work. My brother and I would load hay as the sheep grazed. Those oxen always ran away with the loaded wagon so I, being larger than my brother, would drive. I let them run, guiding them into our hay road. When they came to a hill, they quit running. Then my brother took over and I went back to shocking hay and watching sheep.

Like most homesteaders we had dried cow manure for fuel. We gathered two dozen wagon loads in adjoining pastures and piled the chips in a neat rick which we thatched with sand grass stems to keep the fuel dry. This supply would last all winter as a rule.

Some years our Christmas tree was a post driven into the dirt floor of our house with soapweeds nailed to the top of it. My father called this the Christmas palm.

Hail, blizzard, prairie fire, more hail and still more hail, drove us from our Nebraska home after about 13 years and we moved to south Missouri in 1916.

Elnora Mannon
Brown Branch Rural Station
Ava, Mo. 65608

We Read the Wallpaper

By 1905 a few neighbors had settled in our area and there were school-age children but no school. Some of the parents arranged to set up a subscription school, each family paying one dollar per pupil per month for a three-month term.

The schoolhouse was a one-room frame structure. It belonged to a bachelor who agreed to move in with a nearby family and donate his house to the cause of education.

The teacher was a young man who had only one leg and used a crutch under his arm to walk. That crutch was a thing of curiosity to the children. One day the big boys ran away with it and he begged until they returned it. I cried.

In addition to his small salary, the teacher received board and room. He stayed a week with each family on a round-robin basis. His pupils knew that the week he lived at their house they would be riding to and from school because he couldn't walk any distance on that crutch. When it was our turn to have him at our house, we fixed a cot for him in our small storm cellar. Our one-room dugout was already crowded.

How I loved that school! Our texts were any books that were available—old readers, spellers, whatever we could find. We had an enrollment of eight pupils. My brother and I attended three different subscription schools in three years. We must have been taught well, for when we moved from that area and began to attend regular schools, we were not behind in any way.

179

I might add that we could read before we started to school. Where do you think we learned? Off the wallpaper! Our dugout was lined with cheesecloth, with newspapers pasted over it. A pleasant pastime was looking at the pictures on the "wallpaper" and with some help we learned to read the words.

When I think of all the things we didn't have, I also remember the priceless things we did have. One of these was appreciation for any plaything. For years my brother and I played with a small iron toy, a replica of a man on a cart driving a horse. We called it "Dan Patch." Had it been solid gold, we couldn't have taken better care of it.

I would be untruthful if I said those were the good old days. I certainly don't think they were. For me, these are the good days!

Mrs. Bobbie L. Kennard
Sulphur Springs, Ark. 72768

The Teacher Burped the Stove

I wish some of the kids who gripe about their school lunches could go back to my country school and eat my lunches.

If we were out of butter, we spread our bread with lard and sprinkled sugar over it, or we dug into the stone jar for a piece of fried-down meat to put in our sandwich. We drank water from the well. Sometimes we had cookies or a piece of cake, and now and then an apple.

A large heater stood in the middle of the schoolroom. It burned coal and sometimes would get choked up with coal dust. Then the teacher would open the door, stir the coal with a poker, and the stove would belch out black smoke. We would open the outside door to clear the air.

The restrooms stood in the schoolyard, one for boys in one corner, one for girls in another corner. They were not heated, and if someone forgot to close the door when leaving, you could find snow inside.

All classes were in one room. We learned a lot of things by listening to other classes recite. One teacher taught all subjects to all students. Usually she was the janitor, too, even having to build her own fires unless she was rich enough to hire one of the boys to do it for her.

Mrs. Moody Messick
1501 Alston
Marysville, Kan. 66508

Run, Hen, Run!

One of the small pleasures my father and his brothers enjoyed during their youth in the panhandle of Nebraska was chewing pitch. They picked the gum from trees in a canyon where they went to cut wood for fuel.

My father was chewing his pitch gum in school one day when he lost it to a chicken.

School was held in a neighbor's unfinished house which had no glass in the windows and no door. Chickens wandered in and out at will. When the gum fell from Father's mouth, an old hen grabbed it and ran thru the door, followed by the boy. He pursued the hen around the yard until she dropped the gum. When he had retrieved it, he washed it at the pump and slipped back to his desk. The teacher, busy hearing a little group recite, never missed him.

Alberta Phinney
317 West 3rd Street
Ogallala, Neb. 69153

Schoolroom-bedroom Combination

In the community where my father homesteaded in Yuma County, Colorado, there was no school. Our nearest town was Wray, 20 or 25 miles away, and our nearest woman neighbor was three miles distant.

When I was eight years old, a preacher and his wife took a homestead three miles south of us, and they let a school be set up in their largest room.

181

In the morning they would take down their bed and set up homemade benches. Thru the school day the benches served as desks and seats. In the evening the process was reversed.

We had three months of school that first year. Our teacher was an elderly lady; I loved her very much.

Mabel G. Riddle
Box 124
Reynolds, Neb. 68429

Students Supplied Their Own Seats

A number of homestead families arrived in 1910 and settled in the northeast section of Colorado. By fall of that year a small one-room concrete schoolhouse had been built and enough funds were available to hold school in session for four months of that year.

My father made seats and desks for three of us, but most of the children brought chairs from home and sat at a table.

We studied from our Baldwin readers and other textbooks which Mother had packed when we left our Iowa school.

A teacher was quickly found as an old-maid teacher from Illinois had homesteaded nearby. Miss Rose, the teacher, was a prize taffy-maker, and we enjoyed many a taffy pull in her home and, on special occasions, at school.

Ruby Bigelow
Route 3, Box 3600
Grandview, Wash. 98930

Discipline Was Strict

There were 100 pupils in the Kansas country school I attended in the late 1880s. Some of us sat on boxes. Two classes recited simultaneously, one for the teacher and the second for older pupils who taught the younger children.

During class study, someone passed the water which was taken from a big bucket with a long-handled tin dipper. If that dipper was ever washed, I never knew it.

Order prevailed in the school. We were forbidden to criticize the teacher, a preacher, or any official. If we were punished at school, we knew a similar punishment would be meted out at home.

Did we learn? Out of that school came clergymen, doctors, lawyers, teachers, and good wives and mothers, and so far as I know, not a single criminal.

Eva Vincent
Box 29
Alden, Kan. 67512

CHAPTER 15: Family Tales

Heritage in Family Stories

Treasure your family history! The stories you leave for your children are a far greater heritage than the silver teapot.

Great-grandma often guided our steps toward thrift with a tale of how she brought a single paper of pins with her when she came West; at her death there was still a full paper of pins tho she had used them all during the years she raised a large family.

Then there is the story of the old-timer from the hills who came visiting summer and winter wrapped in a buffalo coat. On a hot July day, Grandma insisted he remove his coat. The old gentleman cleared his throat and said, "It would not be proper. This is my only attire."

How we laughed about the Indian who filched an ornate stovepoker, hot off the grill, and fled thru the trading post leaving a trail of smoke and wild howls.

Then there was the brave dog that carried mail across the bridgeless river and was swept away in high water. Found dead weeks later, he still held his trusted packet in his mouth.

Nellie Duffy
1330 South Grand
Glenwood Springs, Colo. 81601

Indian Headdress

My grandmother tells this story which I understand happened over 100 years ago.

Few possessions could be bought from the motherland when emigrants from Europe moved into Nebraska. But Great Aunt Hester packed, of all things, a huge stovepipe hat!

Every Sunday the hat was taken out and worn to church. The services, held in the open, were watched by the Indians who also noted Aunt Hester's great hat.

One day, when the women were alone, Indians visited the homestead. It didn't take long to discover they wanted no more than the big black hat. Unwillingly, the prized possession was given up.

And then a second Indian indicated he, too, wanted a black hat. Quickly Aunt Hester offered a cast iron kettle as a substitute. The Indian accepted.

The women laughed as he rode away and wondered how he would fare, astride his pony, wearing an iron kettle.

Ang Shonka
1920 South 32nd Ave.
Omaha, Neb. 68105

The First Housewarming

My great-grandmother, 90 years old, tells this story.

When she was a little girl, her family moved from Virginia to a place near Union City, Tenn. Her father chose a site on a hillside for a one-room log cabin, and he built the new house around a large flat rock which would serve as a hearthstone for the fireplace.

On a cold, snowy afternoon in midwinter, the family moved into the cabin, built a fire in the fireplace, and cooked supper. Then the little ones, rolled in quilts, lay down in front of the fire to sleep.

As the fire got hotter, so did the snakes that were wintering

185

under the rock. Suddenly they came out, turning, twisting, and hissing.

The family retreated from the cabin. They slept in the wagon until the day they were sure Gramp had rid the house of snakes.

Randy Dillingham
Kingsley, Mich. 49649

Fire, the Prairie's Worst Peril!

Perhaps it was the talk of others or maybe a pioneer spirit that urged Carrie and Jacob Larabee to set out for distant lands. They journeyed south and west from Iowa, finally finding the right spot, a section of land in Rawlins County, Kansas.

Here they built a sod house along with a cave which afforded protection from storms and storage for food.

Both Jacob and Carrie had had a good education and knew its value for children growing up on the prairie. When a schoolhouse was built about a mile from their home, Carrie volunteered to be the teacher.

Fire was the most dreaded of all the perils of the prairie. One day Carrie and her pupils saw fire in the distance. Somehow she obtained the services of two men with horses and plows and she saw that a wide furrow was plowed around the schoolhouse. The pupils were saved.

But Carrie's own children were at home. She hurried there and rushed her four daughters, aged eight, seven, five and four, into the cave. She saved her daughters but my Great Aunt Carrie was unable to save herself. On that terrible day, May 28, 1899, she died.

After the tragic death of his wife, Great Uncle Jacob took his four young daughters to Nemaha County, Kansas, where his mother and other family members were living. There he met and married Annie Mary Rothline Fikan in the early part of 1900.

Annie had been a normal girl, weighing 85 pounds at age 15. But something happened and she gained weight rather rapidly over the years. She was a happy person and a good stepmother to the four girls.

In 1902 an amusement company asked Annie to join them. Billed as "Annie Redline," and with her husband Jacob as spieler, the girls as singers and doing trapeze acts, the family went on the road.

When "Annie Redline" was 40 years old, she was 4 feet 8 inches tall, weighed 611 pounds, and measured 7 feet 11 inches around. Her arms at the elbow were 34 inches and the calf of her leg was 36 inches. She was on "exhibition" on the Midway at San Francisco, Calif., for weeks and drew a crowd of over 260,000 people.

While on tour at the Columbus, Kan., reunion grounds, Annie contracted malaria fever and died at the age of 44.

Marjorie Kerr Wright
1330 Sherman
Clay Center, Kan. 67432

Early Day Drive-in

My father built a rock house, 16 by 20 feet, with a corrugated roof on our claim which was halfway between Boise City, Okla., and Springfield, Colo. If wagons stopped in one of those towns, the travelers were told they could spend the night at our place and buy milk and bread there.

When it was rainy, people camped at our place for days. The old covered wagons would get so wet that the families would come to our house and sleep on the floor. If several wagons stopped at one time, our floor was covered with pallets. Babies slept on the table.

Mother was known for her wonderful light bread and the wagon people were glad to buy it. One traveler, a very fancy lady, declared she had never tasted anything like it! One day when she came to the house to escape the rain, she watched Mother bake. We had a small two-holed Topsy stove, with an oven about three feet above the stove in the flue. Of course, our only fuel was cow chips. Mother, always careful, wore gloves to handle them; every few minutes she had to refuel the stove.

When that woman realized the kind of fuel we had, she hit the ceiling! She refused to eat another bite of that wonderful bread!

Mrs. Virginia Tucker
Route 2
Elkhart, Kan. 67950

A Stop in Iowa Lasted a Century

In 1870, my grandparents left southwestern Wisconsin bound for the free lands of Kansas. They crossed the Mississippi and journeyed about 50 miles along the old Military Road in northeastern Iowa. Illness among the small children forced them to stop in an area of flat prairie land. Here they stayed for nearly 10 years, turning the tough prairie sod with a breaker plow and ox team.

Grandfather bought a small timber lot in Chickasaw County and moved his family there in 1880. The one-room house on the land was typical of its type: boards on end nailed to a pole frame. The inside walls were covered with successive layers of muslin and paper to close the cracks. A thin board floor did little to stop the bitter winds of winter. The children slept in the loft.

Grandmother carried water from a hole dug at the edge of the slough.

The area abounded in small rattlesnakes. Once when Grandma laid the baby on a blanket between the rows as she hoed the potato patch, she turned to see a rattler slithering toward the child. She killed the snake with her hoe.

Grandfather added small timber plots to his original purchase until he had 80 acres. The land was covered with brush and small trees, and Grandfather cut and sold poles which were used as hoops on barrels. This was the source of the only cash income the family had.

Grandfather moved the house from the field to a location near the road. Moving was a tedious job done with a stump puller and a team.

The family grew and the farm prospered. An addition was

made to the house and a large barn was built. My children are the fourth generation to call the farm home, and our family tenure spans 96 years.

Mrs. Leonard Kristiansen
Route 2
Nashua, Iowa 50658

Animals Rescued From Burning Barn

I had a friend in Nebraska who used to talk me out of a jelly sandwich about two o' clock in the morning—and in return would tell me fascinating tales. I was a nurse's aide, and Mamie was one of 52 patients.

One morning she told me about a barn burned in a prairie fire. "Mama saw the black smoke across the prairie," she recalled, "and she knew there was a fire. She fretted, but the men folks kept saying, 'No, there's no fire,' and they went about their business.

"And then suddenly she saw the blaze shoot over the hill. Their barn was in the path of the fire. The men immediately began making fireguards.

"Mama ran to the barn, and fighting the smoke, untied the family cow. She worked frantically to untie the horse, but the sorrel fought the rope. When she was freed, Old Nel didn't want to leave the burning barn. When at last Mama had pulled and tugged her out, the horse reared and ran back to her smoke-filled stall. Mama gave her last energy to bring the frightened horse out of the barn, and then she latched the door.

"Mama and the cow and the horse all survived the fire, but the great barn was destroyed. It had been built in the canyon with a basement for animals and a second story for hay.

"A barn raising took place later, and a new roof was nailed on the repaired foundation all done in one day. Then the men hauled Mama's organ out to the barn and a fellow brought out his fiddle. Everybody came for a big barn dance.

Mrs. Ethel Simianer
Lowell, Ind. 46356

True Love Found a Way

My grandparents, Andrew Hinshaw and Sarah Ann Hiatt, were married January 7, 1857. The ceremony was performed in a minister's cabin on the bank of the Cottonwood River. It is believed to have been the first marriage known to have taken place in present day Lyon County, Kansas.

Grandmother Sarah Ann had come with her Quaker family from Indiana to help make Kansas a free state. Their wagon train journey took 48 days, from March 25 to May 11, 1856. The route, of necessity, lay thru Iowa as Missourians were unfriendly to free state people crossing their territory. Missouri was a treacherous place for abolitionists at that time.

In spite of chills and fever, mud and mire pools, swollen creeks and changeable weather, they finally reached St. Joseph, Mo. The ferryman pointed to a forlorn-looking old cow tied to a stake and asked Sarah Ann's father what it was. Curtis Hiatt replied, "A cow," whereupon, much to his relief, they were allowed to pass over. Had Hiatt drawled "cayow" as Southerners did, they would not have been allowed to cross.

Grandfather Andrew had met Sarah Ann in Indiana and had preempted land near Oskaloosa, Iowa, planning to establish his future home there. But when Sarah Ann moved to Kansas, Andrew followed.

Leaving Iowa December 5, 1856, he rode by stage to Council Bluffs, Iowa. On December 21 he took dinner with Indian Chief Tongonoxie whose mother, the chief declared, was 106 winters old. Andrew caught a ride to Lawrence, Kan., the next day on a load of lumber. On the way the driver struck a hidden stump and down went his whiskey jug—spilled in the snow! But dog-like, on hands and knees, the driver lapped up enough to make him hilarious before reaching Lawrence.

Christmas Eve was spent at the Council House, Burlington, Kan. The next morning he caught a canvas-back stagecoach for Council Grove. He got off at Withington's on 142 Creek, and after eating, headed on foot for the Hiatt homestead. Caught in heavy rain and sleet, he took shelter in a half-roofed cabin. The next morning he walked to the present site of Emporia State University, spotted a curl of white smoke and hurried to his sweetheart. Altho he had not eaten for 26 hours, he did not eat the two apples he had with him. They were gifts for Sarah Ann when they were reunited December 27, 1856.

Elba Hinshaw Cope
Route 3, Box 148
Hillsboro, Kan. 67063

One Day Late

When he had staked out his farm in the Cherokee Strip, Grandpa returned to Missouri and took his wife and their small children to their new home.

The first child to be born in the Cherokee Strip after the opening was given a gift. Grandma's baby almost won.

I remember Grandpa gesturing with his pipe (loaded with homegrown long green) and saying, "If Dan 'ad been born a day sooner, we would have won the five silver dollar prize." Then he would puff the pipe a little and add, "Yes, sir, that five dollars would'a bought your grandmammy a new dress and a month's groceries."

Mrs. Nelson Cornelius
R.R. 1
Cosby, Mo. 64436

Civil War Gold

Grandmother, who was eight or 10 years old when the Civil War broke out, lived with us when I was a little girl and she told me many war stories. I especially liked this one.

Grandmother's father and his brother came to Missouri from Kentucky and homesteaded adjoining farms. Both had plenty of good land and large herds of cattle, and were considered prosperous in that day.

Missouri, a border state, was overrun by ruffians. "Bush-wackers," Grandmother called them. They robbed Great-grandfather three times, taking everything they could carry from his house. So when Uncle Calloway sold part of his cattle and was paid in gold coins, he showed the money to his wife, then hid it. He never even told his wife where it was.

That night he was called to the door by armed ruffians who had heard about the cattle sale and demanded money. He refused to tell them where it was and he was shot down.

The money was never found. The family was certain the robbers did not find it, and for years people hunted for it. But Uncle Calloway had done his work thoroly.

Ruth Hammock
Laquey, Mo. 65534

Murder at Halfway House

When my grandmother was growing up, her family moved to Meade, Kan., and they were living there when the Daltons were operating the Halfway Eating House in that area.

Ranchers brought their cattle up the trail, past Meade, to Dodge City, and sold them. On the way home, they would stop at the Daltons' house for a meal and rest. Many were carrying large amounts of cash realized from the cattle drive.

While a man was enjoying his food, one of the Dalton gang would reach thru a curtain behind the guest at the table and give him a blow on the head.

A trap door in the floor opened and the rancher dropped into the basement, where he would lose his money—and his life.

A tunnel between the basement and the barn permitted members of the family to pass freely, without notice, from the house to the stall where the victim's horse had been tied, saddled and ready. One of the gang would ride the horse past the Oklahoma border and lose him there.

In the night, the Daltons would bury the victim. A favorite place for hiding the body was the orchard near the house.

So many cattlemen disappeared that lawmen became suspicious and began to investigate. They discovered numerous graves; some bodies were uncovered as far as 20 miles away.

Settlers from all around Meade came to help in the search. One of the volunteers was my grandfather, E. L. Lower.

Mrs. Frances Barnes
315 Cheyenne Street
Canadian, Texas 79014

Clean Calicoes for Sunday

This pioneer story was related to me by my mother-in-law, Mary Jane Ellison Lamont Kitlen, who was pioneer queen at a celebration at Turon, Kan., October 7, 1945.

"I came to Kansas with my parents in 1885 from Illinois. We located 10 miles west of the present location of Turon, but there was no town then. Our mail came by stagecoach once a week from Hutchinson, more than 40 miles away. Several years later a post office was established seven miles from our home and we drove a wagon or rode a horse to get the mail once a week.

"Our first home was one room, dug back in a hill; the front was sod with a wooden door. Our next home was made of wide vertical boards, with wooden battens to cover the cracks. Sometime later Father built a good sod house, with shingled roof; there were two rooms and it seemed really elaborate.

"I remember well the blizzard of 1886. We burned corn to keep from freezing and fat hogs froze in their beds.

"We plowed the sod with oxen, and I walked beside Father, holding a rope tied to the oxen's horns so if they got out of line he could grab the rope and pull them back into place.

"On Saturday we girls washed the calico dresses we had worn all week and had them fresh and clean to wear to Sunday School the next day and to school the next week."

Esther Billings Lamont
Route 2
Nevada, Mo. 64772

Indian Rheumatiz Remedy

My maternal grandparents, who lived in a farming community in southwest Arkansas about 1896, had a son, perhaps 16 years old, who was crippled from rheumatism. None of the three doctors in the county had been able to help him, and no poultice or remedy could ease his suffering.

One day an old Indian, with a pack on his back, stopped at the gate and asked for water. Grandpa, a friendly man, asked him to sit and rest a spell. Immediately the Indian noticed the crippled boy propped with pillows in a rocking chair.

The Indian said he could help him. Grandpa and Grandma gave their consent and the old man went to work, rubbing the boy from his head to his feet. The pain eased and the crippled lad fell asleep.

The old man said he was in no hurry and he would stay and help the boy in exchange for food and a place to sleep. Altho it was considered risky at that time, they accepted his offer. At once he went into the woods and gathered roots and barks to make a liquid which he rubbed on the boy's joints as he massaged him.

After many weeks the patient recovered sufficiently to allow his parents to take charge. The Indian gave his formula to Grandpa; he had to memorize it as it was not to be written. He bade them farewell and they never saw him again.

Grandpa became well known for his Indian Rheumatiz Remedy. He gave it to people who could not pay and made a minimal charge to those who could. He made the medication until he died at the age of 88.

Stella M. Lasswell
11339 Hickman Mills Drive
Kansas City, Mo. 64134

When Ranchers Gave Way to Grangers

Much has been written about the squabbles between settlers and cattlemen as the homesteaders settled on the free range. But my mother and father, who lived in early Nebraska, always spoke highly of the Drydens, the Rankins, the Olives, and other cattlemen who so generously helped them thru those first terrible years when hail and drouth almost drove them back East.

Many pioneers did leave, the signs on their wagon sheets proclaiming, "Going Back to Missouri to the Wife's Folks," and "Goodbye, Nebraska! Hell Must Be Much Like You!" The hardiest stuck it out; some like my mother's parents, the Hunters, were too poor to leave, and home, Pennsylvania for them, was too far away.

The most disheartening time came when lightning struck their little home, killing the baby, Sarah Velma, in her highchair and blinding her mother. After a few weeks the mother's sight miraculously returned and she was able to see the face of her son Roy who was born prematurely that terrible night.

My father's father, Joseph Marcus Chrisman, a Virginia-born man, once removed to Missouri, brought a caravan of covered wagons with family members to Custer County, Nebraska, in the spring of 1882. My father, "Gene," as a boy of 14, rode into the county behind his father's herd of purebred Durham cattle, brought in from Texas.

In that first winter they lost a third of their cattle. The ranchers said of them, "Those Chrismans laid up enough sod that summer of 1883 to fence the county." The tragic lesson from those earlier blizzards taught my Grandfather Chrisman that cattle could not withstand the blizzards of the Great Plains without ample forage and shelter.

The rest of the cattlemen learned that lesson three years later when the blizzards of 1886-7 ended the range cattle industry and opened the plains to settlement by the grangers.

Harry E. Chrisman
10245 West 14th Avenue
Denver, Colo. 80215

Thread Was a Gift of Love

My great-grandmother had a story she loved to tell. The incident she recounted took place in a dry goods store in the early days at Fort Cobb in Indian Territory, now Oklahoma.

Grandie (the family's name for her) was left a widow with two small children. Somehow she managed to support them and to buy a farm which is still in our family.

One day a little girl came into the store with a few pennies she had saved to buy her mother a birthday present. There wasn't much in her price range, but she found something she was sure her mother would like and need. The present? A spool of thread. She was so proud of her purchase.

There have been occasions when my finances prevented my buying something I wanted to give, but Grandie's story reminded me that the meaning of giving is not in the gift but in the thought behind it.

Elaine Millwee Bellamy
Box 394
Fort Cobb, Okla. 73038

They Lived—But Slowly

Shortly before his death, I spent time listening to my uncle, Carl Fuchs, tell about his early days in western Oklahoma. He came to the state in the early 90s, and looked around for a while before he found a place he liked on East Buffalo Creek in what was then Roger Mills County, and he filed a claim.

His nearest neighbors were ranchers, one nine miles east and another 10 miles to the southwest. All was open range and was being grazed by the Long S steers.

Uncle Carl tried to grow a little corn. He said what the prairie dogs didn't eat the Long S steers did. One day when the steers were in his corn he got on an old gray mule he often rode and put on a long linseed-oiled slicker. When he was close to the steers he spread high his old slicker and let out a loud whoop. Those steers stampeded over the hill and when they came to Middle Buffalo Creek where there were only a few narrow trails down the high boxed walls, they just piled off into the boggy creek. Uncle said he didn't go down to see how they all looked in the bog.

Uncle Carl's father, who had been threshing in Kansas, stopped to see him in the summer of 1896. He left the train at Woodward and walked about 100 miles to the Fuchs' place on Buffalo Creek.

After noticing what the hot summer had done to the native pine boards of the house, he told his son he had better fix that place or his wife and babies would freeze when winter came. Uncle admitted there were cracks between the boards that you could throw a dog thru! With his father's help, Uncle Carl managed to haul flat red rocks from about four miles away with which they veneered the house.

When his father was about to leave for his home in Texas, Uncle Carl said, "Pa, why don't you come up here and get a place where the water runs on top of the ground? You're going to starve in that dry country."

Grandpa looked out and saw East Buffalo Creek running cool and clear, and he remembered the four dry years that he and his boys had been hauling stock water with a wagon and barrels. Then it began to sink in.

Maybe he couldn't get the thought of East Buffalo Creek out of his mind, because some time that winter he brought his family and their possessions in two wagons to Oklahoma and settled on Buffalo Creek just upstream from Uncle Carl. One of his six children was Albert who would be my father. He married the year after he came to Oklahoma.

Papa got a job herding sheep over on the head of Starvation Creek. Mama often said the $15 monthly wage didn't go very far in buying supplies. She seemed to miss fruits and preserves most of all. Of course, they had a bountiful supply of wild plums, but sugar was dear and they couldn't afford to buy enough to sweeten those plums to suit her taste.

Papa was very hospitable and never let strangers go by without inviting them to share his humble home. Once he asked two wagonloads of travelers to spend the night. When they drove up and began to pile out, Mama was aghast. Where and how could she bed down 16 people? To feed and sleep that many people in a one-room dugout would scare even a pioneer woman. I doubt if those travelers remembered Papa's hospitality, but Mama did!

Papa decided to grow a money crop, so he planted a patch of

cotton. His neighbors asked what he was going to do with cotton when he got it made since there were no gins around there. When Papa picked his cotton, he had 1,600 pounds which he hauled more than 100 miles to Quannah, Texas, a trip that took him more than a week. I recall hearing many times that the cotton brought about $25.

Yes, they lived then, but they must have lived slowly.

Evan Fuchs
Route 2
Sayre, Okla. 73662

The Day the Earth Turned Black

This is a true story. I experienced it on my folks' homestead near Wallace, Neb., in the spring of 1913 when I was a little girl.

I remember so well that terrible prairie fire. It burned 20 miles wide and 70 miles long, jumping 16-foot fireguards as if they were not there. It was pushed along by a 60-mile wind so it traveled fast.

The day started with a gentle breeze, but the wind grew stronger until it was blowing a regular Nebraska dirt storm. My father had taken Mr. Tucker, a neighbor, and his son to town, and my mother, my baby brother, and I were staying with Mrs. Tucker until he returned.

When the smell of smoke began to drift in on the wind and the day grew darker, the women became worried. Another neighbor, Mr. Hayes, lived about a mile to the north, and Mother and Mrs. Tucker decided they would walk there. I remember trudging along between Mrs. Tucker and Mother, hanging on to their hands, while Mother carried the baby. They anxiously watched the northeast from which the fire would come.

We reached the Hayes' house with not much time to spare, for shortly the coyotes, rabbits, birds, and prairie chickens began to appear around the house, running ahead of the flames. Mr. Hayes thought we should go to the cellar. As we started there, a son of the Ridenhous family came racing in on his horse. He refused to come with us, saying he would jump into the water tank when the fire came close.

Mr. Hayes took a couple of wooden pails of water to the cellar with us. As the fire passed, smoke and sparks poured thru a crack in the cellar wall. We children started choking. Mrs. Tucker and Mother took off their aprons, dipped them in water, and tied them over our faces.

The cellar door was on fire when we tried to come out. The Ridenhous son, who was not harmed by his stay in the water tank, put out the fire. What a bleak, dark world we saw beyond that door!

Mr. Hayes' house, built on a high concrete foundation with tin sides, had very little smoke in it. I learned that day never to leave a house in a prairie fire, for even if it does catch fire one will have time to get out after the grass fire passes by.

Mr. Hayes had 200 white-faced cattle which he had brought from Kansas. He had managed to corral them before we arrived. Of course, his sheds and stacked hay around the corrals were in flames; we saw rabbits, afire, run into the stacked hay. The man would not look toward his corrals, but Mother and Mrs. Tucker persuaded him to help them try to save the cattle. I stood at the house window and watched the women in their long dresses and highlaced shoes open gates and mill those frightened cattle out of the corral and up to the house, saving every one.

With his binoculars, Mr. Hayes began to scan the country. The smoke was so thick he couldn't see a mile, but as it cleared he could spot blazes here and there. He told Mrs. Tucker he believed the fire must have missed her little two-room frame house. That was a surprise, for grass grew almost up to the house. But I've seen fire do queer things; it may be almost to a building, then split and go around it. That's what it did at the Tucker's.

Mr. Hayes told my mother he could see a bright fire at our place.

My father finally came for us and we drove home thru a most desolate country, with posts, cow chips and small animals still smoking and blackness everywhere. At our place, all that remained was the windmill and the little two-room house. A slat corncrib that had held 2,000 bushels of ear corn was a bright red heap of hot coals. At the charred remains of the hay barn we all broke down and cried for the loss of a pet mule for which my folks recently had been offered $15, a lot of money in those days.

All that night my parents packed water to save our little house as the wind switched into the east and blew embers from the hay barn and corncrib toward the house.

The next morning a wagonload of our neighbors drove in and my father asked the men if they had seen his range stock. They dropped their heads and answered yes. "You had better take your gun," they told him, "and finish killing those 28 mares. The mules, all 48 of them, are dead." My father fell to the ground as if he had been hit, and he was in bed for two weeks. The men went back to the mares and shot them for him.

Father had lost all his stock except Babe and Bill, the two horses he had been driving the day of the fire. Within two weeks Babe was killed by lightning, and Bill was struck by lightning and died in the corner of the yard fence.

My father was hit hard by that fire, harder than any of his neighbors, but we were grateful that our lives had been spared.

Nellie Phillips Miller
1623 N.E. Vine,
Apartment 46
Roseburg, Ore. 97470

Some Things You Don't Forget

When Larmon brought Martha
to their prairie homestead,
it often puzzled him
how a man could love a woman so
and always more and more.

Of course there was her beauty,
black hair and slender waist,
but there was something deeper—
caught like the white pattern
in mockingbird wings,
or the red slash of sunrise
in a clouded morning.

Larmon never forgot
the first time he almost grasped
how Marthie, as he called her,
was unusual—special.

The wedding over
they were loading their wagon
for the journey westward
when it became apparent
there wasn't room for everything.
Without protest Martha put aside
quilting frames and chest of linens—
things dear to pioneer brides—
laughing as she said,
"Larmon, my organ has to go even if we have
to leave behind our family Bible!"
He had to widen the dugout door
to get the organ inside,
but Larmon complained only in fun.
That organ sang "Amazing Grace"
for neighbors hungry for a holy word:
"Put Your Little Foot" for dancing
when fall harvests came;
and "The Sweet Bye and Bye"
when their first baby died.

Thru the years they moved
from dugout to three-roomed shack

and finally to a larger place.

The organ always went first load.
"It has to go, that organ,
if the Bible gets left behind,"
Larrnon would say in Martha's voice
so she would turn and smile,
remembering with him.
Oh he loved her—
white spread of wings,
red slash of sunrise.

Long after Martha was gone, and Larmon
in his dotage—people said—
a journalist writing about the old west
asked him, "What about pioneer women—
your wife, what did she do?"
"Well, Marthie played the organ,"
Larmon began. 'I disremember how many kids we had,
but some things you don't forget."

Then he was talking to himself
as neighbors had said he would,
"That's it! I loved her
because of that organ!
Dag-nab-it,
I still ain't saying it right.
Work, drouth three years running,
sick kids and the cow gone dry—
No matter what, Marthie was music,

Marthie was music! . . .
and still is!"

Eyes closed, he smiled
and the questioner was silent

as if he too
heard an organ's
distant playing.
—Mildred Crabtree Speer

(Poem based on true happenings in the lives of Larmon and Martha Crabtree, parents of Mildred Crabtree Speer.)

INDEX

M

N

O

P

Q

V

W

Y